This is Your Life
The Schottenfeld Family Circle

Book by
Louis B. Schottenfeld
with contributions by many others

ISBN Number 978-1-304-74309-1

"This is Your Life, The Schottenfeld Family Circle"

On June 8th, 1980, the Schottenfeld Family Circle gathered in the Avenue Z Jewish Center in Brooklyn, NY to celebrate its 38th birthday. The highlight of the event was the "This is Your Life, The Schottenfeld Family Circle" presentation, modeled after the wildly popular 1950's television show "This is Your Life" in which everyday people were feted with their history and reunions with childhood friends, etc. The committee of Lou and Frieda Schottenfeld (my parents), Ruth and Hy Zudiker, Herb Schottenfeld and Ruth and Nat Levine labored for months to make this an unforgettable event.

Each family member in attendance received a 100-page book, lovingly prepared by Dad with contributions from so many others, containing the known history of this branch of the Schottenfelds. The effort from all was astounding.

Fast forward to the summer of 2013. My daughter Lisa Schottenfeld (now an Oakland, CA resident) attended a seminar in Oakland. Upon noticing her nametag, another attendee told Lisa that her grandmother was born a Schottenfeld. Could they be related? During break time they realized they had common genes when both mentioned the "Schottenfeld Family Circle". But neither knew a lot about the Schottenfeld family tree so they were unable to pinpoint their relationship.

Lisa called me that night, told me about the encounter, and asked if I knew who "Juliana Morris" was. I immediately knew that Lisa had met her first cousin (once removed), daughter of John and Ilene (nee Berger) Morris and granddaughter of Ted and Sarah (nee Schottenfeld) Berger. The "Schottenfeld" family name had worked wonders again; had their last name been "Miller" or "Jones", neither would have ever considered a possible relationship.

In another quirk it turns out that Juliana lives only a few miles from our house in a Boston suburb. With our varying schedules it took some months before we were all able to get together. The "reunion" was delightful. While we got to know each other I pulled out my fragile and yellowing copy of the "This is Your Life, The Schottenfeld Family Circle" book. It saddened me to realize that Juliana, along with dozens of other relatives like her, had never seen it.

With the help of technology, the book you're holding now is a facsimile of the one created in 1980; I've only added book page numbers to supplement the original page numbers. Much has changed in 33 years. Many of the family members mentioned in the book are no longer with us. Many relationships have changed. But many more relatives are now part of the family and this book will provide them with a record of their ancestry.

I hope you treasure the book as much as I do.

Steven Schottenfeld

A Note about the Cover

The 38th Anniversary Celebration was something of a "Bar/Bat Mitzvah" of the 25th Anniversary celebration. The 25th Anniversary celebration was lower key, but a committee did produce a similar - albeit thinner - history book of Schottenfeld Family History for the occasion. That book included the hand-drawn family tree that appears on the cover of this book. The last page of this book contains the full-size version of that family tree.

38 Anniversary Celebration
You are invited to a presentation
of

This Is Your Life
The Schottenfeld Family Circle

June 8, 1980
Starting promptly~1:00 pm.
Cocktails~Show~Dinner

Avenue Z Jewish Center
875 Avenue Z, Bklyn, N.Y. 11235
Tel: NI 6~9874

R·S·V·P. May 15, 1980
Ruth Zudiker ~ Tel: VI 6~3607

June 8, 1980

Dear Friends and Relatives:

I greet you in this fashion precisely because of - and not
in spite of - the old adage, "You can choose your friends,
but your relatives are wished upon you." We are all here
on this happy occasion, celebrating the 38th Anniversary of
our Family Circle, because in addition to being wished upon
each other, we also chose each other as friends.

Incidentally, as you will see and hear later in the program,
we have previously celebrated the Family Circle's Bar
Mitzvah Anniversary as well as our Silver Anniversay. Today
we are marking the Silver Anniversary of our Bar Mitzvah
Anniversary celebration - or is it the Bar Mitzvah Anniversary of our Silver Anniversary celebration? Whichever way
you say it, good friends are always happy to get together -
even if they are related.

As you will also hear later, I have a perfect record of
never having had a movie projector break-down, and I thought
my sole function today would be to run the projectors.
However, the committee insisted that we should start with
official greetings from the President. Of course, as you
will again see and hear later, the last time some of us
received Official Greetings from the President - of the
United States - the results were rather interesting, to say
the least.

Seriously, though, I am very pleased to be given this oppor-
tunity to welcome you all to participate in this Simcha,
and to thank you all for your splendid cooperation in making
your photographs, movie film and slides available for the
program. I am particularly happy to welcome our meshpuchah
from such far-flung places as Florida, Pennsylvania,
Maryland, Washington, D.C., and Poughkeepsie, and I know
you all join with me in sending greetings, love and copies
of this program book to our children in such further-flung
places as Israel, the Mediterranean, Mexico, Los Angeles,
Chicago, Rochester and Boston. Who would have believed it
when we first started, and when the furthest fling then was
between Brooklyn and the Bronx!

Finally, and most importantly, I want to give credit where credit is really due. Later on in the program, Louis is going to insist on thanking, and maybe even praising, the members of the committee, other program participants, and our hosts and hostesses for making all of this possible. Yes, we did work hard, and will work even harder today to make this a success, and we thank Louis in advance for his kind words. However, the real credit and thanks must go to Louis himself. The very inspiration for this enormous and time-consuming undertaking belongs to Louis. He created the format, he wrote every word, he selected every picture, he designed and even typed every page of the program book - in short, he recreated every loving memory we are about to be privileged to re-live and which we will be able to treasure in book form forever. With your help, Louis has done what every museum curator dreams of doing - he has put together a once in a lifetime showing of a collection of priceless pictures and word pictures. Louis calls it, "This Is Your Life - The Schottenfeld Family Circle", but as you are about to see and hear, it is much more than that. It is really Louis' version of our "Roots" - although in our family as you know, and are about to be reminded by the program, it might be more appropriate to say, "Ruths". I know each of us is about to shed some tears for loving memories, just as I know we will also cry from laughing so hard. Louis, you may have been wished upon us, but each and every one of us also chose you, and loves you, as a dear friend.

And now, let's go back in time - in the same way our Family has always gone forward - together!

                    Love,

                    Herb

PRESENTING
****

"THIS IS YOUR LIFE"

THE SCHOTTENFELD FAMILY CIRCLE

JUNE 8,1980
at the
Avenue Z Jewish Center
****

...And thus begins the saga of the SCHOTTENFELD FAMILY CIRCLE.

Yes, to answer the question of "Why is this organization different than most others?" How come the SCHOTTENFELD FAMILY CIRCLE survived the war years, differences of opinion, mixed ages of members, and why wasn't it affected by boredom, apathy and personal frictions that usually beset other such organizations?

The answer is simple. Our parents loved and were concerned about each other. They would visit frequently. In those days, children went where their parents went, and thus the children got to know each other imtimately, and cousins became part of each other, sharing secrets and growing pains.

Yes - who can forget the good times we shared with each other. The births, the briths, the birtdays, the Bar Mitzvahs, the Bas Mitzvahs, the Weddings, the parties, the get-togethers and the planned meetings.

We would sometimes do crazy things at parties, like the skits on Purim or Chanakah, or the yacht trip, or the ball games pitted against the Neuwirth Family, or the picnics and bowling meets.

We did hundreds of things together.

Happy events were the engagement announcements, the graduations and accomplishments of our children.

The births of our grandchildren. Ours, because we felt we were part of one. The "nachus" of becoming a grandmother or grandfather, had to be shared with all members.

At 'Honor Nights', 'Testimonials' and 'Installations' all of us would "shep nachus" because the person being honored was one of ours.

And celebrating our own birthdays, anniversaries and special events, sometimes by just wishing each other well by singing Happy Birthday or Happy Anniversary, sometimes by elaborate parties - they were always fun times.

Yes, the good times were wonderful, but we also had bad times. We had our share of sicknesses, hospitalizations, operations, family problems, and to some, the unfortunate passing away of loved ones. Through them all, there was always a SCHOTTENFELD around to help ease the pain.

We shared the good times and we shared the bad times. We comforted each other when comforting was needed. We were more than just related to each other - We were a Family.

When a part of our family is happy - we are all happy.
When problems beset a part of our family - we are all unhappy.

Yes - but most important. we were very fortunate. We selected and married spouses that were just like us.

That is why - THE SCHOTTENFELD FAMILY CIRCLE is different than most other organizations.

-1-

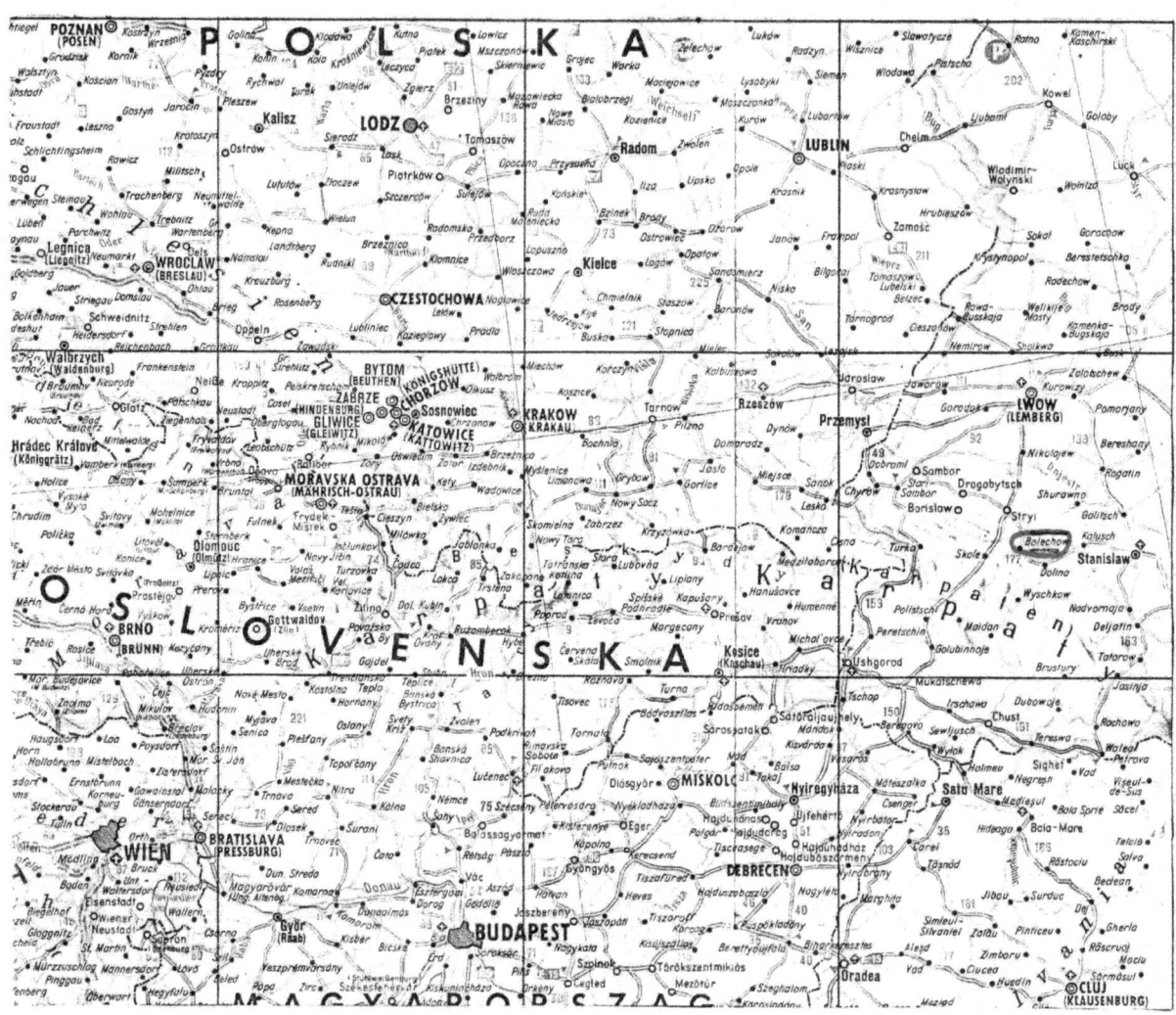

In order to better understand the makeup of the SCHOTTENFELD FAMILY CIRCLE, it is necessary to go back 100 years.

Yes, the year is 1879. Ruchel Hauptman and Hersh Schottenfeld were married in Bolechów.

Bolechów, in those days, was under the control of Austria-Hungary and after World War I became Poland again.

Life in Bolechów was not as bad for Jews, as in other European towns and cities. Of course, there was a great deal of anti-semitism, but not to the extent of the pogroms of Russia, or the fierce hatred of Jews by most other peoples of Europe, which often led to their expulsion, or living in fear of beatings and harsh laws against them.

After the year 1750, the Nobleman, who was given a charter to settle the area in Galicia which included the town of Bolechów, invited Jews to settle there, promising them they would have the right to own property, have religious freedom, and in a few towns, such as Bolechów, even have the right to have a say in the election of a Mayor. Police had an obligation to protect Jews.

Many of the Jews who came to settle, were from Vienna, where oppression was great. It is very possible that the Schottenfelds that settled in Bolechów came from Vienna. There is a family of Schottenfelds in Cincinnatti, whose ancestors are from Vienna. There is, at present, a street called Schottenfeld G asse, in what was once the Jewish section of Vienna. A woman we met in Israel, who came from Europe during the war, claimed to be a member of the Vienna Schottenfelds. She mentioned names that coincided with our family names. However, Frieda and I suspect the Schottenfelds took her in as a baby when the Nazi's arrested her parents, and took care of her until they were taken away. She showed us an old family portrait (the father was a spitting image of Uncle Willie) but kept by-passing our question as to why she wasn't in it. We felt she wanted to belong to some one, and perhaps knew nothing of her real parents, or family name. We did take her and her husband out for an evening of fun. It was all the time we had. The manager of the Hotel Zion in Haifa knew the Schottenfelds very well and became very excited to hear we were Schottenfelds, even though not from Vienna.

Which leads us to believe that our family, about three or four generations before Hersh emigrated from Vienna. Unfortnately we have found no evidence that any Schottenfeld survived the Holocaust in Europe. A Bolechówer who miraculously escaped to Russia and was saved by Bernard Semel in 1947 told me that he had been through many camps and parts of Russia, and never came across any Schottenfeld that was still alive.

By 1879, Austria Hungary was ruled by Franz Joseph. The Jews of the Town of Bolechów were allowed freedoms that were unknown in other parts of Europe. Many Jews served in the Army.

However, by 1890, the people started hearing of gold that covered the streets of America and also parents dreaded seeing their sons drafted into the Army. The threat of insurrection and wars was in the air - so - emigration to America began in earnest.

Yes,during the next 16 years,after their marriage, 5 chidren
were born to Hersh and Ruchel Schottenfeld:

...VELVIL (2nd from left) in 1880

...Isaac (far left)   in 1882

...ISRAEL (center)   in 1887

...SELIG (far right)   in 1892

...FEIGA (2nd from right)in 1896

Yes,born during those years,are children,who are later to marry
the Schottenfeld brothers and sister:
Fanny Brown is later to become the bride of Velvil.

Pippa Hirshout is born in Bolechow. Her name at birth and until she
is 10 years old, is Libba. A younger brother,as a child, cannot say
Libba, but pronounces it Pippa. The name stuck and no one ever again
calls her by her correct name. She later becomes the bride of Isaac.

Pippa is born in the year 1889.

Fanny Jampel was born in 1890 and becomes the bride of Moshe later in life.

Fanny Newirth is born in Bolechow in the year 1893 and after
coming to America ,she becomes the bride of Selig.

Max Kornbluh is born in Bolechow on March 24,1892,and after coming
to America,he marries Feiga.

Morris Greifer who is later to marry Feiga Kornbluh,when she
remarries, is born May 1,1890.

Yes,the year is 1904. Velvil was the first to come to America.
It is not clear as to what motivated the move.It proved to be
a fortunate decision. It had to take a lot of courage and much
heartache to leave ones parents and loved ones behind.The brothers
and sister Schottenfelds,all emigrated soon after,found new lives ,
settled down,married and had children. The sad part,is that so
many of our brethren , did not leave and later could not.

Velvil became Americanized,changed his name to William, and to
make a living,he became a wholesale bread distributor-using a
horse and wagon to make deliveries to stores.

3

William was a handsome man and married Fanny Brown, and they became parents of 4 children:

Arthur (left of picture)
Louis (right of picture)
Ruth
  and
Nathan

About the year of 1930, after the passing away of Fanny, William married Anna, and two more children were born, a daughter named Jean and a son named Harold. Anna also has a daughter Elsie, who marries and has a daughter Susan. Jean marries Jack and have Laura, Kathy and Billy. Harold marries Elaine, and their children are Steven and Jan.
William was usually a mild mannered man and a great charmer. But, he had his moments of stubborness and could be very opinionated. When aroused, he could go into blind fury and was noted during these moments, for backing up his horse and wagon into a stream and dumping his cargo of bread into the water.

Later, he opened and operated an automotive tire store at different locations, 18th Ave and 84 Street, 18th Ave near 86Street, and Utica off Church Ave. He became very ill- and passed away in 1941.

His son Arthur, had various jobs. He worked for his father, was a presser in a garment factory and later had a laundry route. He married Bessie, a public school teacher. The marriage produced two daughters, Elaine and Linda.

Williams son, Louis, was a good looking young man. He was very protective and concerned about his sister Ruth and his brother Nat. He became interested in the Order of DeMolay, an arm of the Masonic Order. He was rapidly working up the chairs. Unfortunatly, he was killed while working for the Mason and Hanger Corporation, building an East River Subway Tunnel. A chunk of red hot steel got into his shirt and stuck at his belt line. He rolled in the dirt, and no one around him knew what was happening. Fearful of him getting the bends , they couldn't get him out of the tunnel in time.

Daughter Ruth worked for the telephone company for many, many years. She married Lou Whitman, who was a plumber. But, rather than do plumbing, he loved building racing sail boats. Once, he didn't measure right, built a boat in his basement, and then had to chop down an entire wall of their home to get it out. He was awarded many championship cups. Ruth and Lou have two children, Robert and Joan.

Son Nathan, as a child, unfortunately caught Polio during the epidemic of 1918. He remained in braces, walked with crutches and used a wheelchair to get around. He was a brave, bright young man, and was always self sufficient. He was an avid philatelist, president of the stamp club at New Utrecht High, and bought and sold stamps. As a youngster, he opened a small printing shop and ran the press. He met and married Cappy, who took wonderful care of him. They lived in New Jersey, where he was a radio announcer.

4

For some reason, none of the children (their father William had already passed away) ever showed a desire to join the family circle organization. Occasionally, we would meet at an affair, but that was it.

After Arthur passed away, his wife, Bessie, showed some interest, joined the organization and came to meetings. But, she too, suddenly passed away, and then nothing from her children. Sometimes not even to acknowledge a gift we would send for a birth.

Yes, the year is 1903. Twenty one year old Isaac leaves his job in a Bolechow leather factory, because he is drafted into the Austria Hungary Army. He is to spend the next 3 years of hiis life there.

Yes, the year is 1906. Israel says good bye to his family and leaves for America. Upon arrival, he Americanizes his name to Morris, and to conform with that name, he becomes Moishe. No one ever again calls him Israel or Yisrael. The only remembrance is when he gets an Aliya and is called to the Torah. The Synagogue calls on him to fix things, and even though they rarely can pay him, he never says "no". To make a living, he becomes a carpenter, joins the union, and becomes a strict union member for his entire working years. On the job, his co-workers call him Charley. When times get tough, he would rather not work, than take a non-union job.

Yes, it is April 27, 1907. Born to the Kessler family in Poland, is a son who is named Jack, at his Brith on May 4th. He doesn't know it then, but, after coming to America, he is to meet and marry Ruth Schottenfeld (Pippa and Isaac). In America he makes a living selling dry goods, then goes into manufacturing childrens pajamas and then gets into ladies pants.

5

Yes, it is Jan.
of 1908.
Isaac and Pippa
are married in
Bolechow.

Yes, it is December 18, 1908. There is great
excitement in the Isaac and Pippa household
in Bolechow. A first child is born. They
name her Ruth.

Yes, the year is still 1908. Selig says
good bye to his family in Bolechow and
comes to America. He is 16 years old.
The first thing he does, is Americanize
his name to Jack. He becomes better
known as Jake. His first job is in a leather
factory. He then tries to become a
plumber, then tries his hand as a subway
builder. Finally gets back to the leather
business, his first love.

6

Yes, the date is Oct.1,1910. A second child
is born to Pippa and Isaac Schottenfeld in
Bolechow. At his Brith ,he is named William.

*note-on picture William is on right.
             next to him Uncle Jake and Artie.

Mr. and Mrs. S. Jampel

Mr. H. Schottenfeld

request the pleasure of your presence at the marriage
ceremony of their children

Fanny Jampel

to

Morris Schottenfeld

on Saturday, June 17th, 1911,

at 8 P. M.

at Vienna Hall,

105 Montrose Avenue,
Brooklyn, N. Y.

Bride's residence,
616 a Willoughby Ave.
Brooklyn, N. Y.

Yes,it is the spring of 1911.Invitations are
sent out for the forthcoming wedding of Fanny
Jampel and Morris Schottenfeld.

7

Yes, the date is June,17
1911. Fanny Jampel becomes
Mrs.Morris Schottenfeld.
She is a gorgeous bride.
Moisha,is a master crafts-
man in carpentry.

Yes, the date is Aug.17,1911. Jack Teller
is born in Lotz,Poland. When he is 3 years
old,his family emigrates to America. He is
later to marry Ruth Schottenfeld,daughter
of Fanny and Moisha.

Yes, she refuses to tell us when,but,during
these years Lilian Povidlo (later to become
the wife of William) is born.

Yes, the year is 1911. Fifteen year old Feiga,
tearfully says good bye to her family in Bolechow and comes to America.
She Americanizes her name to Fanny and goes
to work in a factory as an operator. She
works near the Triangle Shirt Factory and sees
the tragic fire. She remembers for the rest of
her life, the girls jumping out of windows.

8

Yes, the date is Apr.19,1913. A third child
is born to Pippa and Isaac in Bolechow.
At his Brith he is named Arthur.

Yes, the year is still 1913. There is a great amount of unrest
in Poland. A war is imminent. A decision is made. Isaac is
to leave for America as soon as possible, leaving Pippa and the
children behind, to see if he can make a living in the new country.
He gets a job doing carpentry work in a subway construction job.
Carpentry is not his forté, but is advised by his brother Moishe,
to put a board on his shoulder and carry it from one end of the
job to the other. He does this and gets away with it for quite
a while.
At Castle Garden, the Admission Officer, puts his name down as
"Eisyk" (a phonetic spelling of Isaac), and for the rest of his
life he spells his name that way.

Yes, the date is Nov.12,1913. Ted Berger is
born in New York City. At the age of 7 he
goes to Czechoslowakia, where he is to attend
school. In 1930, when he is 17, he returns to
America. He is later to meet Sarah Schottenfeld
and they are married.

Yes, it is January of 1914. Isaac gets lonesome for his family,
and writes Pippa that he is returning to Bolechów to be with
them.
Pippa sends back a letter not to come, but to send them a Visa
to come to America. They arrive at the end of January.
Arthur, the baby, is now 9 months old. They get here just in time.
War soon breaks out in Europe, and all emigration ceases for the
duration. They find a placeto live on Bay 14street in Brooklyn.

9

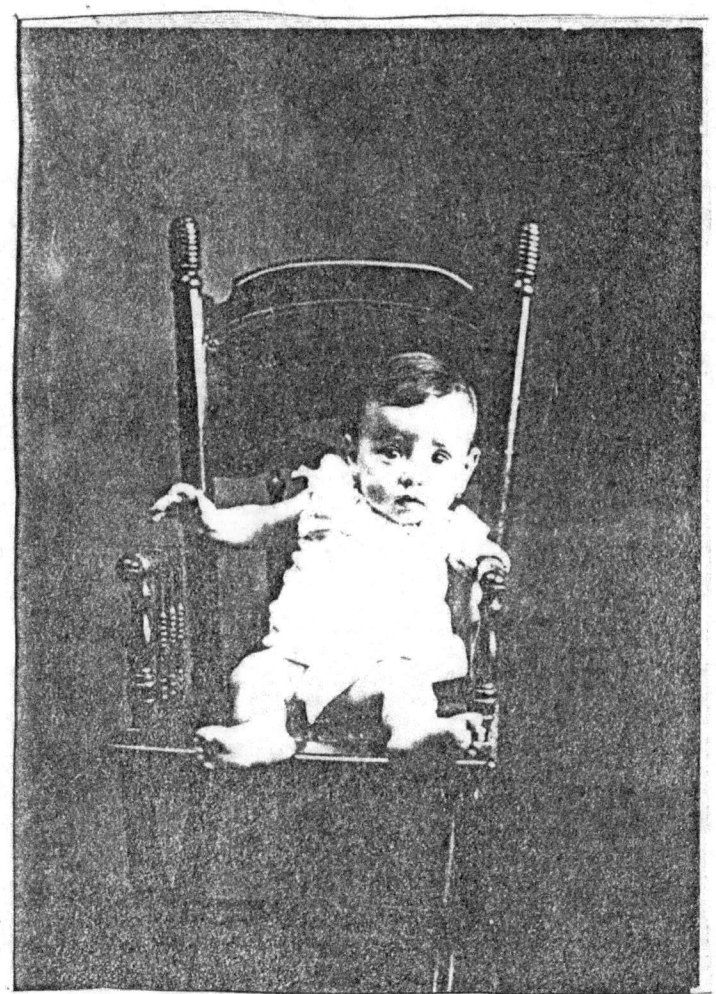

Yes, the date is
March 20,1914.

Fanny and Moisha
become   proud
parents, their
daughter is named
        Ruth

Yes, the date is September 15,1915. Nat
Levine is born. He doesn't know it yet
- but he is to later meet and marry
Ruth Schottenfeld, daughter of Fanny
and Jake.

10

Yes, the date is Dec. 5, 1915. Lillian Brooks is born. She doesn't know it yet, but later in life she is to meet and marry Arthur Schottenfeld (Pippa and Isaac).

Yes, the date October 10, 1916. Pippa gives birth to a fourth child. The first in America. At the Bris, Isaac and Pippa name him Louis.

Yes, the date is April 5, 1917. The Zudikers have a brand new son. They name him Hyman. He doesn't know it yet, but he is soon (about 25 years later) to meet and marry Ruth Kornbluh.

Yes, it is still the year of 1917. Feiga Schottenfeld and Max Kornbluh are married. Max is a wonderful man. He is a waiter and then opens his own restaurants. He works very hard. Feiga helps him in the restaurants. Ye editor remembers him as a kind, jovial person. As a child, I was taken to his restaurant on Spring Street, by my father and Uncle Jake. It, being my first restaurant, I was flabbergasted by being asked what I would like to eat. All I could say was Milk and Cookies, which brought great laughter to my father and Uncles.

Their home was like a restaurant. The first thing you did when visiting, was to eat. Even though, economically, things were very rough at times, Fanny never let on, at the table.

ii

Yes, it is January 10, 1918. A second child
is born to Fannie and Moisha Schottenfeld.
They name their brand new daughter Gertrude.

Yes, it is March 23, 1918. A first child
is born to Fannie and Max Kornbluh.
At his Brith on Mar.30th, they name him
Sidney.

*note-Sid is on extreme right. Posing
      with him are Artie, Lou, Hannah
      and we can't figure out who is
      the kid in front of Sid.

Yes, the date is April, 20, 1918. Tess is born.
She doesn't know it at the time, but,
she is to become the bride of Sid Kornbluh
later in life.

Along about this time, we know
the date is Sept.13, but we are
forbidden to mention the year,
Frieda Wilansky is born in the
Bronx. Her mother grooms her
from birth, to get a fellow and
get married. Later in life, her
friend Ruth Schottenfeld (Fanny
and Jake), tells her about this
cousin in Brooklyn, named Lou.
They are to meet and marry.

12

Yes, it is Nov.24,1918, and Sarah becomes the
fifth child of Isaac and Pippa. The next day
a great dinner was held. We still don't know
if it was in honor of the birth of Sarah or
Thanksgiving.

*note-Sarah on extreme left- to right of her
            Mom ,Hannah and Harry

Yes, it is Dec. of 1918. Fanny
Newirth becomes the bride of
Jack Schottenfeld. It is a lovely
marriage. Their home becomes a
focal point for visiting from
both sides of the family. It is
like Times Square. If you wanted
to see anyone, you didn't have to
call them up. Just go to Fanny
and Jake and the odds were that
the person would be there.
Ye editor, used to love to visit.
First the train ride (one BRT-
and than two IRT). Then came the
good stuff. My Uncle Jake would
take me to the local candy store
(downstairs) for a chocolate malt-
ed and then feed nickles into the
pinball machine, so I could play.
He was a champ at it. He could
rock the machine without getting
a tilt.

Yes, it is Oct.20,1919. A first
child is born to Fanny and Jake.
They name their daughter Ruth.

Yes, the date is Dec.15,1919. A second child
is born to Fannie and Max Kornbluh. She is
a beautiful daughter, and they name her Ruth.
This completes a cycle. All first born daughters of the off-spring of Ruchel and Hersh
of Bolechow are now carrying the name Ruth.

Yes, the date is April 19,1920. Harold
Diamond is born in the Bronx. He doesn't
know it yet, but later in life, he is to
move to Poughkeepsie, where he is to meet
Shirley Kornbluh and they are to marry.
Shirley is to be born in Brooklyn.

13

Yes, the date is June 27, 1920. A third child is born to Fannie and Morris. They name their beautiful daughter Mildred.
At the age of 1, Malkie went on a diet.
    Proof----->

Yes, the date is June 23, 1921. A sixth child is born to Peppa and Isaac. At the Bris they name their new son, Harry. The family now lives at 8615-17 Ave.in Bath Beach. The huge house becomes the center of activities for the entire Schottenfeld Clan. Those, who are privileged to be old enough to remember the warmth of the home, the fun of living there, and the unforgettable years which would take a whole book to describe, still talk about it.
As soon as Harry sits, without crying, we pose for a family portrait.
   *
   note Back Row- Left to Right Bill,Pop,Ruth,Mom,
                                                Artie
        Front Row   "   "   Harry,Sarah,Lou

Yes, the date is June 6,1923. Danny Levitz is born. He is not aware of it yet, but, later in life, he is to go to a USO Alumni Dance, where he is to meet and later marry Hannah Schottenfeld.

14

Yes, it is Sept.20,1923. Hannah is born.
She is the 7th child of Pippa and Isaac.
Sarah gives a sigh of relief, because   the
rules of the house, specify, the youngest
girl child, washes the dishes. No way does
Hannah abide by that rule.
She also remains the baby of the family,
as Pippa and Isaac say "thats it " .

Along about these years, a daughter is born
to the Leo Heisler Family. They name her
Florence. We know she was born on Dec.5th,
but she declines to tell us the year. She
does admit to being born before 1930. Anyway,
she is later to becomethe bride of Harry.

Yes, itis March 1,1924. A second child is born
to Fannie and Jake. At his Brith, he is named
Herbert. His present pot belly suggests that
he was weaned on malteds.

Yes, it is Feb.11,1925. A third child is
born to Fanny and Max Kornbluh. They name
their brand new daughter, Shirley. She is
a "bren" as a child , and never changes.

*note-Sonny snuck into this picture.That's
            him in the middle.

Yes, it is the year of 1925. Tragedy strikes the family. Max
Kornbluh, at the young age of 33 years, passes away.Feiga is
left with an infant and 2 young children. Only her courage,
her love for her children, and the concern of the family,
keeps her going.She conquers, and as soon as possible, takes
jobs as a waitress and bakery saleslady, to bring up the
children.

15

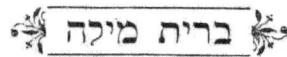

Mr. & Mrs. M. Schottenfeld

Request the honor of your presence at the
Circumcision

ברית מילה

of their new born Son

On Saturday July 17th, 1926, 3 P. M.

at their residence

8726 - 17th Avenue   Brooklyn, N. Y.

Yes,it is Jul,10,1926.A fourth
child,a son,is born to Fannie
and Moisha Schottenfeld. At his
Bris, on July 17th,he is named
Sidney,but,by that time his parents
already call him "Sonny",because,
the sun rises and sets on this kid,
and he is spoiled rotten by Fannie
and Moisha.

*note-The mail must have been better
 in those days.Imagine,within a 7 day
 period,to be able to get cards prin-
 ted and mailed,in time,for an invi-
 tation.

In the 20's ,photographers
went around with a horse,
and took baby pictures.
Here is Sonny on one,
but he not entirely
fearless. Note the photo-
graphers assistant hiding
behind the horse. His job
is to keep the horse
from moving.

Yes,it is now July 25,1928. A lovely daughter
is born to the Balters. They name her Lorraine.
She doesn't know it at the time,but,she is to
marry Herbert Schottenfeld,when she grows up.

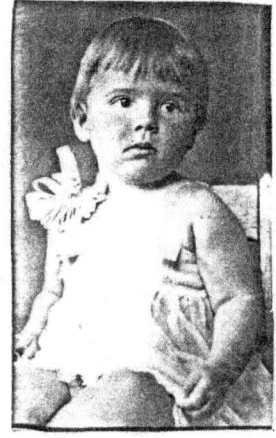

16

Yes, the date is May 31,1929. Elayne is
born. She finds out later in life that
she is to become Mrs. Sonny Schottenfeld.

Yes, it is Oct.18,1931. Ruth Schottenfeld (Pippa
and Isaac), gives up her job at the Bensonhurst
National Bank, and with Sonny as flower boy, she
is married to Jack Kessler, at the DeLuxe Palace.
Counting Hersh and Ruchel as the first generation,
this is the first of the 3rd generation of
Schottenfeld weddings. It sets a pattern. It
is a stomping affair , as are all future ones.

Ye editor remembers the affair very well. I was
in charge of seating people. In those days, people
didn't think it was so necessary to answer that they
were coming (there were no stamps on the return
card), but they did show up. So, whoever, came over
to ask where they were sitting, and finding I did not have their
name on the seating list, I told them TABLE 13. There was only one
trouble, there was no TABLE   13 . So you can imagine the chaos
when everyone was told to find their seats, and 32 people were
wandering around looking for Table 13.
But, with all that-Ruth Schottenfeld that day became Ruth Kessler.

Yes, it is the year 1932. Tragedy again strikes the family.
Fanny (Moishes) passes away at the young age of 42. The family
is stunned. She looked so well at Ruth and Jacks wedding, no one
can believe it.
The family is strengthened in its sorrow. Ruth assumes the duties
of a mother. In the intervening years, Gertrude and Mildred dedicate
themselves to the care of their father.
Moisha argues frequently with the children, but, fiercely loves
and is devoted to them, and would kill to protect them if necessary.

17

Yes, it is Feb. 20, 1934. A son is born to the Rosenfelds.
At the Brith, he is named Ronnie. Later in life he is
to become the husband of Faye Kessler.

Yes, it is July 23, 1934. The Pippa and Isaac household has become a bedlam. The first miracle was
the parting of the Red Sea. The second is the
birth of Faye to Jack and Ruth Kessler. The first
grandchild.

Yes, it is still the year of 1934. The Povidlo's
(Lil is later to become Lil Schottenfeld) have
a son. They name him Jerry.

* note- on the photo-sister Carol.

Yes, it is July 3, 1935. Irving Weiss is born. He
doesn't know it yet, but he is later to become
the husband of Carol (daughter of Bill and Lil).

Yes, it is 1936. William Schottenfeld marries Lillian Steck.
She is to pass away later and Bill remarries.

Yes, it is June 27, 1936. Danny Levitz becomes a Bar Mitzvah,
but, still doesn't have even an inkling that later on he will
marry Hannah.

18

Yes, it is June of 1937. Feiga Kornbluh meets
and marries Morris Greifer. The family moves
to Poughkeepsie, where Morris has a newspaper route. Morris has 2 daughters, Sarah
and Rose and one son, Aaron, who is married
to Rita. They have 2 daughters, Roberta and
Margaret.
Years later, Morris and Feiga are to move to
Brooklyn, where Morris opens a liquor store.
Morris becomes very active in the Flatbush
Park Jewish Center.
*note-on photo with Feiga and Morris, is
    Hy Zudiker. Center Shirley and Ruth . Bottom Tess.

Yes, it is one minute before midnight on
Dec. 31, 1938. Born to Jack and Pauline
Rosenblatt , is a son they name Joel Sidney.
He claims the distinction of being the last
child born in the year 1938. His father is
very happy, but, we do not know if its because
of Joel or he can claim a last minute deduction,
on his income tax. Anyway, later in life, Joel
marries Diana Kessler.

Yes, it is Mar. 5, 1939. a 2nd child is born
to the Povidlo's. Lil is not yet a
Schottenfeld. They name their new daughter ,
Carol.

    * note- Mom and Jerry get in on the
        picture.

Yes, it is Sept. 10, 1939. Today Ruth
Schottenfeld (Moisha's) and Jack
Teller are married. Jack is with
the U.S. Postal Service. They are
to live in Brooklyn, and make a
lovely couple.

19

Yes, it is May 27,1939. Arthur Schottenfeld marries Lillian Brooks.
It seems Art saw her knock out some guy,with a right to the jaw,and
fell for her muscles.Lillian is a bookkeeper in a sportswear house
and Art is Assistant Manager of American Mdse.Co.

Yes,it is August 20,1940. Ruth Kornbluh and Hy Zudiker are
married.Hy is a pocket book repair expert,and becomes known
as the best in the business.

20

Yes,it is Nov.16,1940.Lou Schottenfeld and Frieda Wilansky
are married.Lou almost misses the affair. He came very late.
Frieda gets nervous and thinks she should start looking around
for a substitute. You see,it was busy at the station,and then
he had to go home to dress,and go to get the liquor (in those
days ,who heard of floating bars with mixed drinks). It was the
obligation of the groom to bring the bottles (each table got a
bottle of rye and a bottle of scotch),and that was it. Of
course you had to watch the waiters,who would try to snitch the
the liquor,when they would clean off the dishes from the tables.
Anyway,he comes just in time for the wedding procession. Ruth
(Fanny and Jake) is Maid of Honor.

Yes,we go back 2 months. We knew the year,but just found out the
date. It is September 15,1940. Sidney Kornbluh marries Tessie
Waxman. They settle in Brighton. Sid is a tool maker,in a machine
shop. Tess is a manicurist. After the marriage,Sid feels he
is entitled to a free nail job. Tess tells him to clip his own.

21

Yes,it is January 18,1941. Ruth Schottenfeld (Fannie and Jake),
becomes Mrs.Nat Levine. They met at afurrier manufacturer,where
Ruth worked in the office. Nat also worked for a furrier. He used
to call on Ruths boss,and one day,saw this good looking chick
in the office,decided to tell her the joke about the 2 minks.
One joke led to another,and Ruth thought him tremendously funny.
So,before he knew it,it was Jan.18th and he was standing under
a Chupa. Maid of Honor ? You guessed it- Frieda.

Yes,it is February of 1941. Ted Berger (who
still hasn't met Sarah) is inducted into
the army. He becomes an interpreter and is
shipped to Europe. He is to stay in the army
until his discharge in Dec.of 1945. (He had
a choice ?).

Yes, it is
the summer
of the year
1941. We do
not yet have
a family
circle,but,
we all make
up to meet
at the Hud-
son Day Line
and take a
boat to In-
dian Point.

We

We have a heck of a good time on the boat,
all agree,"We must do this more often."
We practice softball for a few innings. This is to come in handy
for future games with the Newirths.

22

Yes, it is the summer of 1942. The Schottenfeld Clan has one of
our informal get-togethers at the home of Pippa and Isaac.
After a repast of Potato Progen (which Pippa used to whip out
by the thousands), and sour cream, we retire to the front parlor
at 7706-20th Avenue, for jokes, gossip, etc.
In the course of conversation, someone suggests we form a family
circle organization.
Present are Uncles, Aunts and cousins.
It is decided , that if anyone is interested, we will meet at
Ruth and Hy Zudiker in July of 1942 , for further discussion.
By the next meeting, on Aug.26,1942, the Family Circle is firmly
launched.
We adopt by-laws, elect officers, collect dues and get down to
business. Part of the adopted by-laws, limit the membership to
the offspring and their children and their Childrens children
etc., of Ruchel and Hersh Schottenfeld of Bolechów. This ruling,
is to be challenged more than any other, in the intervening years,
as other Schottenfelds not in that catagory, think we are
trying to act very uppidy by excluding the rest of the family.
Actually, we passed it that way, in order to limit the membership
to a small enough number, that would make it less unwieldy and
more manageable.
At the beginning, our aim is strictly social.

And so begins, the next phase. Actually , nothing changed. With
the formation of the Schottenfeld Family Circle Organization,
we continued with what we always did. We always met and visited
each other. Except now, we have planned meetings, planned get
togethers, planned discussions. We did all this before, but on
an informal basis.

Yes, due to the minutes of the first 14 years, and for periods
during the intervening years, missing in entirety, much of what
is part of this evenings program is from memory or tie-in with
some pictures that were taken.

We are sorry to have to leave out so much that is part of the
history of the Schottenfeld Family Circle. We would have liked
to be able to say it all.

If by chance, we leave out an event, a   birth, a wedding or anything
of interest, please excuse us.

We would like to thank those who supplied us with information,
films, movies and slides, which served to refresh our memories
of events. The response to our request was overwhelming. If we
bothered you by phone to get information, please excuse us and
we thank you all, for making this evening possible.

Early meetings had hosts and hostesses supplying coffee and cake.
Before we knew it , we were getting Coffee, cake, bagEls and cream
cheese. Later came bagEls, cream cheese, lox, herring, coffee and cake.
Still later came hot dishes and meats. Than came catered-in meals.
But all this evolved, because of the Schottenfeld spirit of, "if
you come to my house, you have to eat". Refrigerators as well as
their hearts are opened up.

23

Yes, it is Dec.27,1942. We have our first planned activity together.
We have a most enjoyable bowling match at tha Jewish Community
Center.

Yes, it is the meeting of Jan.31,1943. A decision is made to
give family gifts for marriages, births and military inductions.
Due to events of the next 2 years, this decision keeps our
treasury in a near bankrupt position.

Yes, it is Feb.of 1943 . We go to see our first show. It is called
"Show Time". After the show, we have a meeting on a street corner,
to decide "where do we eat". This proceedure is to continue for
many years, until it is decided,   "where we eat" at the meeting,
before the show.

Yes, the year of 1943 was a catastrophic one for the Schottenfeld
Family Circle. The organization was only a few months old, when
members began getting induction papers.

Yes, it is Apr.3,1943. Lou Schottenfeld leaves for
Camp Upton. After basic training, he is sent to
Ordnance School at Aberdeen Proving Grounds and
then transferred to the Engineers and sent to
Ft.Belvoir, Va. He is to see service in the South
Pacific. He gets discharged in July of 1946

Yes, it is MAR of 1943. Herb Schottenfeld is
inducted into the Air Corp. He is to see service
in Italy. He gathers more medals than can fit on
his chest. Everytime a plane belonging to his out-
fit, flew over a target, he is awarded another
medal. He still claims he was shortchanged by 14
medals.
He is to be discharged in 1945.

Yes, it is June of 1943. Bill (William)
Schottenfeld is inducted into the army.
He is assigned to the Infantry Military
Police. He is to see service in the
European Theatre of War. He is at the
Battle of the Bulge. He receives his
discharge in Oct.of 1945.

Yes, it is June 20,1943.
Shirley Kornbluh today becomes
Mrs.Harold Diamond. They are to
set up home in Poughkeepsie,
and make a lovely couple.

27

Yes,it is August of 1943.
Daniel Levitz,who has not yet met Hannah,
is inducted and shipped to Camp Crowder,Mo.
In basic,he earns the SHARPSHOOTER medal,and
wears it proudly.He is to become a crew member
of a small army vessal,and sees service in the
South Pacific. He is to receive a discharge in
February of 1946

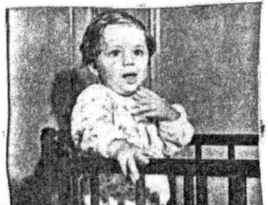

Yes,it is Aug 10,1943. The Kudish family
welcomes a new addition to the household.
They name their new son,David. He doesn't
know it then,but later he is to marry
Naomi Schottenfeld.

Yes,it is September of 1943. Siney Kornbluh is inducted
into the Army. He is soon to be named Casey Kornbluh, as
he becomes a railroad machinist.He surprises Lou by calling
him from Arkansas (Lou was in Texarkana),which was not far .
Sidney is discharged at the end of 1944.

Yes,it is still Sept of 1943. Hyman Zudiker,is inducted into
the Army. He is assigned to the Ordnance Department. He is
to be shipped to Europe. In England he breaks a foot,and
winds up in a hospital,where he has a great time. He is to
show how he feels about being in the Army,by sending Lou letters
with many deleteable adjectives. He must have tought the
censor a few choice words.
A big thrill is,Bill on a truck going one way and him in another
truck going the other ,somewhere in Germany.
Hy receives his discharge in November of 1945.

Yes,it is still 1943. Sidney (Sonny) Schottenfeld
is inducted into the Air Corp. He is shipped to
Utah and really roughs it.The sands of the desert,
keeps blowing into his eyes. Also,he likes his
steak 'Medium Rare',and the cook only knows how
to broil it 'Well Done'. This burns him up,so he
goes to town every night and has his dinner in a
fancy restaurant. Sid gets his discharge in Nov.of 1945.

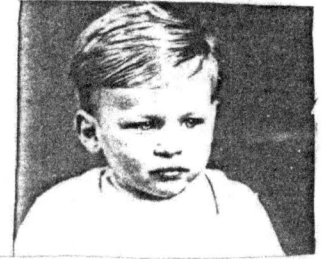

Yes,it is Nov,7,1943. A first child is born to
Ruth and Nat Levine. At his Brith,they name their
son,Barry. Their is lots of excitement in the
home of Fannie and Jake Schottenfeld. Barry is
their first grandchild.

Yes,it is Dec.25,1943. A second child is born
to Ruth and Jack Kessler. They name their
beautiful brand new daughter,Diana.

25

Yes,it is Feb.1944. A decision is made at the meeting,to suspend
having Family Circle meetings, until every is home and all babies,
already started,are born.There are too many of the men in the
service,and the pregnant women are very busy.

Yes,just because meetings are suspended,it does not mean that
events cease to happen to the members.In fact,things warm up.

Yes,it is April 6,1944. A first child
is born to Ruth and Hy Zudiker. At the
Brith,he is named Michael.
He poses with Grandma Feiga.

Yes,it is May 10,1944. Born to Shirley and
Harold Diamond is their first child . At
his Brith,they name him Merrill.

Yes,it is June 9,1944. Richard Zusman is born. He doesn't know
it yet,but,later in life he is to meet and marry Ronnie Zudiker.

Yes,it is Sept.24,1944. Sid and Tess
Kornbluh,become the proud parents of
their first child. At his Brith,they
name him Martin.

Yes,it is Oct.31,1944. A daughter is
born to Ruth and Jack Teller. Lovely ,
Phyllis is to be their only child.

26

Yes,it is Nov.26,1944. There is much joy in
the Art and Lil Schottenfeld household. A
daughter is born this day. They name her Naomi.

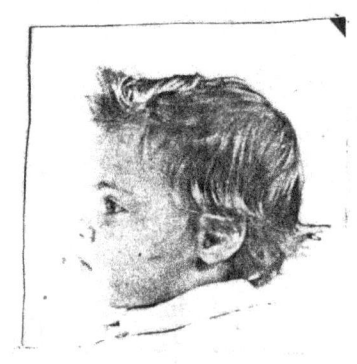

Yes,it is December 3,1944. Harry (son of
Pippa and Isaac) Schottenfeld and Florence
Heisler are married. He works for the
Signal Corp,at Ft.Monmouth,New Jersey.

Yes,it is April 13,1945. Gail is born. She doesn't know it yet,
but,later in life she is to become Mrs.Barry Levine.

Yes,it is May 14,1945. Marc Graber is born. He also does not know
it,but later in life he is to marry Sherri Levine.

Yes,it is the end of 1945. The men of the Schottenfeld Family
Circle,start trickling back from the wars. Thank G_D, they are
all to come home. Some have internal ailments,due to bad food
and harsh weather,but generally , all physical accidents have
healed, mentally they are fine,andall are to return to their
families in good condition. Again Thank G_D.

Most resume their pre-induction jobs,as soon as possible, and it
is as if nothing happened. In fact,some have broadened their
vocabulary. They have learned new words. Most are not in the
dictionary.

Meetings are not resumed for awhile,but,we do a lot of visiting,
to catch up . The new babies born are gorgeous. Ex-servicmen
tell each other ,how they won the war. Funny stories are told.

Nature is wonderful,not so long ago, they didn't tell jokes.

27

Yes,it is Oct.5,1946. A second
son is born to Tessie and Sidney
Kornbluh. At his Brith on Oct.12,
he is named,Alan.

Yes,it is Oct.20,1946. This is the first meeting,after the war
time suspension. A large crowd shows up. There are many new
members of the Schottenfeld Family Circle (a little young but
still members). Diapers go like mad. Everyone is trading
information of Diaper Services. Many women are pregnant.
It is just a wonderful , happy meeting.

Yes,it is Nov.8,1946. Mona is born today. She doesn't know it yet,
but, later in life , she is to become the wife of Michael Zudiker.

Yes,it is March 2,1947. The family does something ,which becomes
a precedent until the present day. We vote to support the UJA
and help the establishment of a State of Israel. When the new
state is founded the next year , we rejoice,and keep sending
funds,to help in protecting her borders.

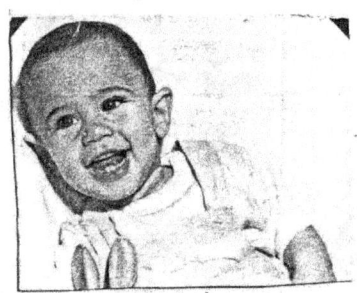

ALAN

Yes,it is March 23,1947. Frieda and Lou
Schottenfeld gaze lovingly at their brand
new number 1 son. They soon find out that
he is a great kid, except he hates to sleep
and loves to cry at night. They take turns
rocking him all night.
But,later in life,things even out. His
daughter gives him the same business,as
an infant.

Yes,it is May 23,1947. Born to the Shuster family is a girl. They
name her Aileene. Later in life she is to go to Puerto Rico for
a vacation,where she meets Alan Schottenfeld, and soon after that
they are to marry.

28

Yes, it is May 29, 1947. Born to the Karp Family
is a son. At his Brith, he is named Ronnie.
As of this day, he doesn't know it, but later
in life he is to marry Judy Levitz.

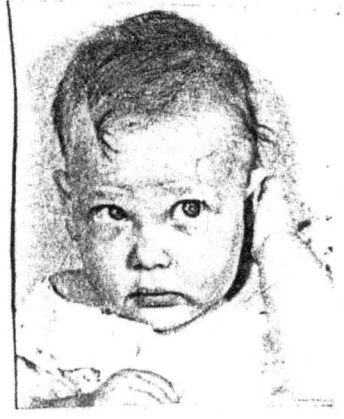

Yes, it is Feb. 19, 1948. A second child is born
to Ruth and Nat Levine. They now have a
beautiful daughter, and name her Sherri.

Yes, it is Feb. 22, 1948. Harry and Florence
Schottenfeld are blessed with their first
child, a daughter, and name her Susan.
Harry goes home early every night to be
with her.
Lou is left to slave away at the service
station.

Yes, it is March 6, 1948. Hannah Schottenfeld
and Daniel Levitz are married. The marriage
culminated from a chance meeting at an
alumni USO dance after the war.
Brother Lou and Ben Newman, at the wedding,
think up a gag that would liven things up.
When everyone is seated, Ben goes outside,
takes off his jacket, rolls it up to make it
look like he is carrying a baby, then enters
and runs up to the main table yelling, "Please
Hannah, come home, the baby needs you".
Of course, Danny and his family, did not know
Ben Newman, and just stood still, with their
mouths open, horrified.
Well, the "shidach", almost busted up right there.
The only one in the audience, who thought it was
funny, was Lou, who was rolling in the aisle
laughing.
Which proves a point, 'What is funny to one,
doesn't necessarily have to seem funny to
others '.

29

Yes, it is April 13,1948. Natalie is born. Later in life she is
to marry and become Mrs.Martin Kornbluh.

Yes, it is April 23,1948. A second child is
born to Ruth and Hy Zudiker.
They name their brand new daughter, Ronnie.

Yes, it is Sept.19,1948.
Herbert Schottenfeld
and Lorraine Balter
are married.Herb is
an accountant and att-
ending law School.
Lorraine is a teacher.

Just as important that
the family circle is
fortunate in adding
Lorraine to the family,
her mother ,Pauline,
becomes one of us.She
is a delight and we look
forward to greeting her
at every meeting and
event. Mrs.Balter is a
wonderful addition to
the family.
*note-on photo with
Pauline Balter. Right-Ruth Kessler.Left Tanta Fannie.

Yes, it is March 22,1949. A second
child is born to Shirley and Harold
Diamond in Poughkeepsie. They name
their daughter,Stephanie.

*note- That's her mom on the photo,
       making sure she doesn't fall
       off the horse.

30

Yes,it is March 24,1949.Hannah and Danny
Levitz greet their new born daughter and
name her Judy. Their first born is a beautiful Child.

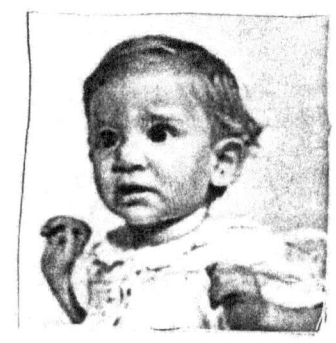

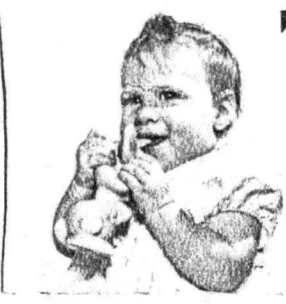

Yes,it is April 6,1949. Today a second child
is born to Arthur and Lillian Schottenfeld.
They name their new daughter,Rosalind.

Yes,it is May 29,1949.
At the meeting held at
Art and Lil,we celebrate
their 10th Anniversary.

The children line up on
the couch and pose for a
shot.
*note-left to right
     Naomi,Diana,Faye who
     is holding Susan,
     Mishael who is holding
     Ronnie,Barry who is
     holding Sherrie and
Alan taking up the right end.

Yes,it is July of 1949. The family circle goes on a picnic,and
we have a great time.

31

Yes,it is Dec.10,1949.
At the 1948 Passover Seder of Pippa and Isaac,
in order to have some fun, Artie convinced Sarah
that if she ate the Hard Boiled Egg,that was part
of the Seder Plate,she would come to the next Seder
as a married woman.
Sarah fell for it and ate the egg.
At the Seder of 1949,Art. again suggested she eat the egg.
Sarah told him to get lost,as the only thing she
got out of eating it last year,was a "farshtopt
mugen" (stuffed up stomach).
Arthur convinced her that custom dictated,that if
it doesn't work the first time,it will work the 2nd.
And it worked. Today Sarah becomes Mrs.Ted Berger.
Ted works for Cohn,Hall and Marks. They met at a
resort,when both were on vacation. He liked the
way she snapped pictures.

Yes,it is Aug.17,1950. Tess Kornbluh
does not fool around with giving birth
to daughters. Today a 3rd son is born
to Sid and Tess. At his Brith ,they name
him Gary.

Yes,it is Sept.24,1950.Sonny Schottenfeld
marries Elayne. Sid makes the decision because
he loves her and he is also tired of hearing
his father call him a "bum",for bumming around
with his friends.
Then again,she's a Dental Ass't,and he figures
he could use her talents on his teeth.
Sonny is also a comic.He laughs himself silly.
Especially,the time that Elayne moves the bed
to another part of the room without telling him,
and he jumps in the dark room,thinking it's
where it always is,only to almost kill himself when he hits the floor.
In time,he is also to get accustomed to eating the odd food Elayne
cooks for him,like, asparagus,topped with egg shells,garnished with
bread crumbs,dipped in honey and the whole thing steamed until soft.

Yes,it is October 5,1950. A 3rd
child is today born to Lillian
and Arthur Schottenfeld.
At his Brith on Oct.12th, he is
named,David.

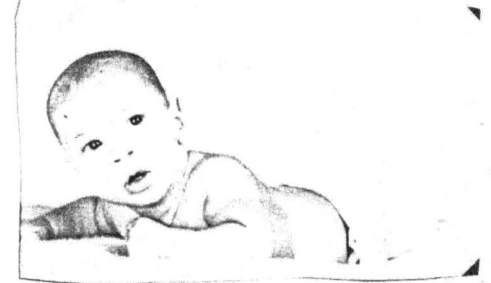

32

Yes,it is the meeting of Mar.19,1951. A most important meeting.
An allied organization is formed.It is called The Schottenfeld
Family Circle Cemetery Organization. Its purpose- To purchase
and maintain a family cemetery plot,for the members .
Not all of the members of the Family Circle subscribe.Some members
already have plots with other organizations,some are pessamistic
as to whether we will pay it off,and some have already purchased
plots. However,most members sign up.
In time, a 72 grave plot is purchased at Beth Moses Cemetery in
Farmingdale (which we cut down to 68 graves in order to allow a
more individual grave size). A family headstone is erected. The
plot is paid off. Shrubberies enclose the entire plot.Perpetual
life care is arranged and paid for. Rules and regulations concerning
the family plot operations are signed by all. Herb is to do a
great job as administrator. Cemetery trustees are elected. Yes,it
all started on March 18,1951. A most important day.

NAOMI SUSAN ROZ JUDY

FEIGA
FANNY
PIPPA

Yes,it is June17,1951.We go to Belmont State Park for a picnic.
Everyone has a great time.

HERB UNCLE JAKE

TED DANNY

ART ROZ JUDY HANNAH NAOMI

DANNY FEDDIE HY

33

Yes, it is June 24,1951. Son number 2,is born to Frieda and Lou Schottenfeld. At his Brith they name him Stephen. Frieda is to stay in the hospital for 5 days,and Alan and his dad have a great time. They eat frankfurters 3 times a day for 5 days.

Yes,it is July 28,1951.A daughter is born to the Florek family. Rose and Murray name her Joan. Later she is better known as Joni. Still later she is to become the bride of Steve (Stephen) Schottenfeld (Frieda and Lou).

Yes, it is Aug.26,1951. Charlene (also to be known as Sherri),is born. She doesn't know it yet,but,she is later to marry Alan Kornbluh.

Yes,it is December of 1951. Joel Rosenblatt,who is later to marry Diana Kessler,becomes a Bar Mitzva.

Yes,it is July 13,1952. Born to the Schwartz family,is a son they name Alan. Later in life he is to marry Roz Schottenfeld.

Yes,it is July of 1952. The Family Circle ,goes on a picnic. Everyone has a great time.

Yes,it is Aug.3,1952. Today,Bill Schottenfeld Remarries. His bride is Lillian Moskowitz Povidlo. She has 2 children,Jerry and Carol. Lil is very lovely and the family welcomes her and the kids into their midst.

Yes,it is Jan.5.1953. A 2nd child is born to Hannah and Danny Levitz. At his Brith on Jan .12th, he is named Fred. His yell is so lusty,the opinion is,from this can only come a Chazan.

34

Yes,it is January 25,1953.A decision is made,that due to crowded
conditions at meetings at members homes,we will rent a room at the
Fraternal Clubhouse. We continue this until evicted,because the
building goes commercial.

Yes,it is Feb.22,1953. The Trachenberg Family welcomes a new child.
At his Brith they name him Teddie. He doesn't know it yet,but, later
in life he is to meet and marryCarol Rosenfeld.

Yes,it is March 1,1953. Karen is born. She is later in life to
become Mrs.Merrill Diamond.

Yes,
it is
June
1953.
We go
on a
Boat
Ride
and
pic-
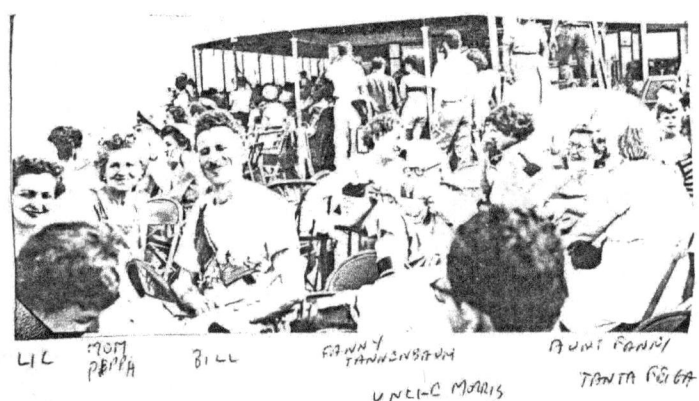
nic in Bear Mountain. It is a gorgeous day and we enjoy.Fanny
Tannenbaum and daughter (cousins) join us.

SARAH   RUTH KESSLER
     JUDY

SID   HERB

UNCLE JAKE PIPPA RUTH KESSLER
     HERB

35

RUTH KESSLER
DIANA?
FAY

yes, we are still on the
boat ride and picnic in
Bear Mountains.

JACK KESSLER
RUTH
JUDY LEVITZ

Yes, it is Sept.22,1953.Today a first child is
born to Lorraine and Herbert Schottenfeld.
At his bris on Sept.29th,he is named Michael.

ISAAS   PIPPA

Yes, it is Jan.3,1954.
At the meeting we
celebrate the 46th
Wedding Anniversary
of Pippa and Isaac
Schottenfeld.

ART   JACK
PIPPA   YL

36   FRIEDA   UNCLE JAKE

Yes, it is May 16,1954. The family selects as a picnic site, the Bronx Zoo. We have lots of fun. The kids have the most fun.

Herb feels bad because we weren't able to recruit even one new member there.

Yes, it is September 9,1954. A first child is born to Sarah and Ted Berger. At his Brith he is named Eugene. Only his parents are to call him Eugene, everyone else calls him Gene.

Yes, it is Nov.27,1954. Faye Kessler and Ronnie Rosenfeld are married. The festivities are very lively and jumping.

Yes, it is Jan.16,1955. We celebrate the 13th Bar Mitzva year of the Schottenfeld Family Circle. Herb and Lorraine compile a journal for the event. It is read , but not published until many years later. By that time the journal is a classic, and copies sent to everyone are treasured.

37

Yes,it is May 26,1955. Elayne and Sidney
Schottenfeld welcome their first child.
She is a lovely baby and they give her
a delightful name, Faith.

Yes,it is Aug.31,1955. A tragedy strikes the family.We all mourn
the loss of Isaac Schottenfeld. He never really recovered from
a prostrate operation. we are to miss him,a wonderful husband,
father and grandfather. He is buried on the Family Circle Plot.

Yes,it is Dec.30,1955. Today a first child is
born to Faye and Ronnie Rosenfeld. At his Bris
on Jan.6th,1956,he is named Harvey.

NOTE - PHOTO - POSING WITH SISTER CAROL

Yes,it is Jan.8,1956. The family circle has a Mah Jong and Card
Party after the meeting. The best part is listening to Jake Schottenfeld

and Morris Greifer,verbally go at each other, as each accuses the
other of playing close to the vest,and only staying in when he
has aces backed up.

THE KORNBLUHS
MARTY   GARY   ALAN

Yes,it is the March 4,1956 meeting.
We take time out for Sarah to snap
some pictures.

PIPPA
NOTE - PHOTO - UNCLE JAKE TANTH FEIGA
AUNT DANNY   UNCLE MORRIS

THE LEVITZ FAMILY
DANNY FRED JUDY HANNAH

33

Yes,it is still the meeting of Mar.4,1956. In addition to posing
for pictures,a committee of Sid,Dan,Hy and Lou,is formed to purchase
and plant shrubs on the family circle cemetary plot. We get up real
early Sunday morning, and select Sid,whose middle name is 'Shrubbary
Maven', to lead us to a plant nursery. Unfortunately, Lou is given
the scissors for trimming them. After planting,he (Lou),trims with
wild abandon.The other committeemen do not know it was a frustration
with him,he always wanted to trim bushes,but never had the chance.
Anyway,all our work is in vain. The shrubs never grow. Lou's excuse -
Sid picked out Dwarf Plants. But,who knows.

Yes,it is April 27,1956. Pamela is born. She doesn't know it yet,
but,later in life,she is to become the wife of Harvey Rosenfeld .

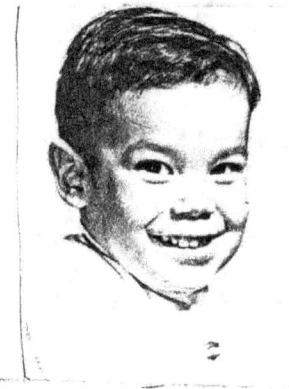

Yes,it is May 14,1956. Today a 2nd child is
born to Lorraine and Herbert Schottenfeld. At
hid Brith on May 21st,he is named Steven.

Yes,it is May 27,1956.we have a delightful outing and picnic at
Belmont State Park. Hy and Ruth Zudiker volunteer to get there
early,to reserve our section and tables. Hy stays outside to
guide us to the picnic spot.

Yes, it is Nov.of 1956. Barry Levine becomes a Bar Mitzva. It
is a lovely reception.

Yes,it is December of 1956. we have a Chanukah Party for the
children. They have a wonderful time and the adults also enjoy.

Yes,it is Feb.10,1957. At the meeting Nat and Ruth Levine show
movies of Barrys' Bar Mitzva.It is greatly enjoyed.

Yes,it is April 7,1957. We have a Purim Party.Lots of booths for
the children. Adults also play the booths and get the least number
of prizes. They miss like mad.

Yes,it is April of 1957. We go to see "Funny Face" at Radio City
Music Hall. We then go to eat,but know not where (it is not in the
minutes).

Yes,it is April 20,1957. A brother is born to Susan
Schottenfeld. At his Brith,on April 27th,Florrie and
Harry,name him Eric.

Yes, it is May 12, 1957. A report is made at the meeting, that a sum of $11.50 was collected in pennies, at the booths the previous month, and was sent to Youth Aliya, in Israel.

Yes, it is May 2, 1957. We attend the Bar Mitzva of Michael Zudiker. Everyone has a great time.

Yes, it is still May of 1957. Merrill Diamond becomes a Bar Mitzva, in Poughkeepsie.

Yes, it is June 23, 1957. we spend the day with the Newirth Family Circle, at Klodes Hotel. We have a competative soft ball game. The food is delicious. Everyone enjoys.

Yes, it is still 1957. Joel Rosenblatt, not yet married to Diana Kessler, joins the Air Corp. He is to spend the next 3 years there. Some soldiers are discharged with medals. He gets out with a cup (for playing football with the championship base team).

Yes, it is Sept. 15, 1957. The Family Circle presents Lou Schottenfeld with a 2 volume Bible Set. Lou is thankful and is honored to receive the gift.

Yes, it is Oct. 11, 1957. A second child is today born to Faye and Ronnie Rosenfeld. They name their brand new daughter, Carol.

40

Yes, it is October, 1957. We join with Tess
and Sidney Kornbluh, in celebrating the Bar
Mitzva of their son Martin. It is a joyous
affair.

Yes, it is Oct.27,1957. Some families gather together at 11 AM, and
take their kids to Cowboy City. They have a rip roaring time .
Lots of shooting. The stage coach robbery is very realistic.

Yes, it is Dec.8,1957. We hold a Chanukah Party. The children are
asked questions and receive lolly pops for correct answers. The one
with the most pops gets a big prize. We have records and play music.
Herb brings a projector and we see an Abbot and Costello Film.
A great day.

Yes, it is March 2,1958. We have a Purim Party. The kids go home with
hundreds of prizes. We celebrate the 10th Wedding Anniversary of Hannah
and Danny. We take in $17.00 in pennies at the booths, and send the
money to Youth Aliya in Israel.

Yes, it is March 30,1958. Ruth Levine reports that she signed a
contract for a family dinner at Phil Glucksterns. We hire an
accordionist.

Yes, it is May 9,1958. Today, a 2nd child is born to
Sarah and Ted Berger, They name her Ilene.

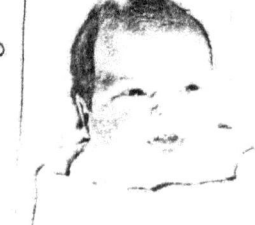

*note- photo taken when Ilene is 6 hours old,

ART   HANNAH   SARAH

HANNAH
WARSAVZKI   LIL   AUNT SABINA   PIPPA
(woman of Pippa)   (SISTER-IN-LAW
                     OF PIPPA)
                     FROM CARACUS,   41
                     VENEZUELA

Yes, it is June 22,1958. We have
a record 40 people of our family
who join with the Newirth family,
for a days outing at Klodes Hotel
in Mt. Freedom, New Jersey.
We beat the pants off the Newirth
team at softball, but not fair and
square as their best man, Mels' son,
is on our team.
It is a great day and we have a
great time.

Yes, it is July 29, 1958. A second child
is born to Elayne and Sidney Schottenfeld.
They name her Ellen.

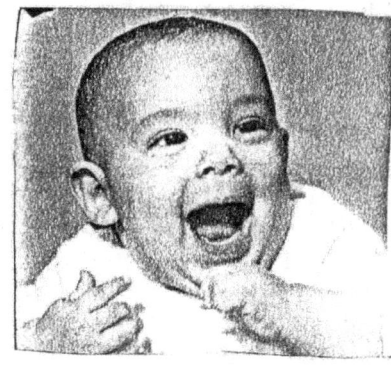

Yes, it is August 19, 1958. Today a 3rd son
is born to Lorraine and Herb Schottenfeld.
At his Brith on Aug. 25th, he is named Matthew.

Yes, it is Nov. 9, 1958. We meet at the Mid-Island Bowling Alley.
We have a bowling match. Cups are awarded to the winners. All
have a good time, even those who do not bowl . They just root
for their favorites.

Yes, it is Dec. 7, 1958. We have another delightful Chanukah Party.
The same questions, the same lolly pops, the same complaints from
the kids that they are not called on to answer when they know that
one, but, we have the same fun.

Yes, it is Jan. 4, 1959. A motion is made and carried, that we save
for a 18th Anniversary celebration.

Yes, it is Feb. 14, 1959. We attend the theatre and see "Majority of One".
Something new has been added. Instead of gathering on a street corner
 to decide where we eat afterwards, we make a decision at the meeting
that we will go to Ratners. Takes all the fun out of blocking a
street corner for ½ hour.

Yes, it is April 5, 1959. Our Purim Party is a great success. We rent
2 rooms and the kids wreck both of them at the Fraternal Clubhouse.
They also go to work on a 3rd room occupied by another family circle,
who think they are being invaded by Martians, and run home early.
A Sum of $10.43 is collected at the booths in pennies, and is forwarded
to Youth Aliya in Israel.

Yes, it is May 1959. A decision is made that a headstone inscribed
with the family circle name and also all family members names,
along with 2 benches, be purchased and have erected at our family
cemetary plot at Beth Moses. A sum of $1025.00 is alloted.

42

Yes,it is June 21,1959. We again go to Klodes for the day. we
have a great time and the kids love it. We again beat the Newirths,
by a one run margin,but this time win fair and square.

Yes,it is Oct.,1959 . We celebrate the Bar Mitzva of Alan Kornbluh.
It is a lovely reception and we all have a great time.

Yes,it is Nov.1,1959.At the meeting,Lou is presented with a set
of Machzerim for his efforts on behalf of the Family Circle. He
thanks everyone,and says he loves doing things for the organization.

Artie is selected to buy a coat rack,which we will store in the basement of the Clubhouse.This is to avoid all the cleaning bills we
have as a result of the coats falling off the chairs at regular
intervals.

A motion is made to look into the planting of shrubbery again.
A suggestion is made that the cemetery ,this time, supply and
plant them. Danny ,Sid,Hy and Lou ,who are very sensitive,are
hurt,because they are not asked to do the job.

Yes,it is Nov.21,1959. A trgedy again happens. Our Uncle Moisha
(Morris Schottenfeld) passes away. We are all grieved. We purchase
trees that are to be planted in his memory,in Israel,through
Keren Kayemeth L'Israel.

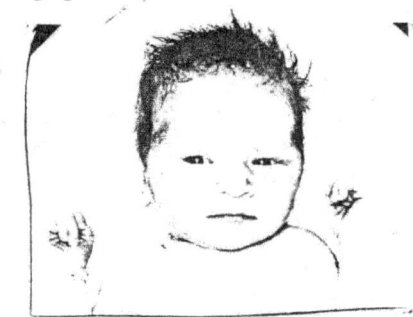

Yes,it is Dec.1959. A   child
is born to Jerry and Isabel Povidlo.
At his Brith,he is named Arthur.

note* photo-he poses with brother
              Michael.

Yes,it is Jan.3rd 1960. We have a childrens Chanukah Party. Same
questions,same wise guy answers from adults,same lolly pops,same
genius kids that win the big prize for most correct answers.

Yes,it is March 6,1960. We go to Arales in Queens . The dinner
is good and the entertainment is excellent. All enjoy.

Yes,it is March 14,1960. Hannah and Danny Levitz
welcome their new daughter.They name her Fay,

    *note-photo- Fay is just hours old.

43

Yes, it is March 26,1960. Alan Schottenfeld
is a Bar Mitzva. His reception is a stomping
affair. It lasts until the wee hours of the
morning. At 3:30 AM breakfast is served.
His brother Steve sleeps through it all.
The next morning Frieda and Lou know why.
He comes down with the measles.

Yes, it is April of 1960. The Purim Carnival is a great success.
The kids put on costumes. We have childrens games. We also have
booths. Ten Dollars is collected at the booths in Pennies. The
money is sent to Youth Aliya, so they too can celebrate Purim.

Yes, it is the May 1,1960 meeting. Artie reports that cloths racks
are 6 Feet high and we would have a storage problem. We go back to
putting our coats on chairs, and pick them up every 10 minutes
from the floor.
The family circle presents Lou with a set of gold cuff links and
tie clisp. Very lovely.
Phyllis makes a complaint that teenagers are not given enough
recognition at meetings. It is decided to revise the constitution
to include children and encourage teenagers to conduct some meetings.

Yes, it is May of 1960. Ronnie Karp, who has not yet
married Judy Levitz, becomes a Bar Mitzva.

Yes, it is June 4,1960. A discussion develops about members who
keep coming later and later, to meetings, causing them to be opened
late and rushed. A suggestion that latecomers be fined, is knocked
down. It ends when everyone says they will come on time.
Congratulations are given to Unle Jake on his official retirement,
from the leather factory.

Yes, it is still June 1960. We go to Messers for an outing.
Klodes is closed. We again beat the Newirths in the annual
softball game. The reason is, that Mel gets a sprained foot early in the
game, when our 2nd baseman blocked the bag, and he had to slide around
him. The Newirths suggest that we did it on purpose, to assure a
win, but we wouldn't do that, would we?
Max Newirth gives a party for his daughter and includes us. It
was a swell party.
Even though it is a bit cool, some brave the weather and go swimming.

44

Yes, it is July 26,1960. A fourth child is born
to Lorraine and Herbert Schottenfeld. They
now have 4 delightful sons. At his Brith, he
is named Howard.

Yes, it is Oct.9,1960. The teenagers were asked to come to this
special meeting for them. They are to elect officers and plan on
doing things, by splitting up into a younger and older group, and
will go out on the town.

Yes, it is the meeting of Nov.1960. A complaint is made that our
president gets no respect. We talk without permission, and hold
conversations with each other. It is decided to have more respect
for the president.
The teenagers elect officers: Pres.   Barry Levine
                             V.Pres. Alan Schottenfeld
                             Sec'y   Diana Kessler
They plan their first outing together- A Movie on Broadway
We enjoy the Sweet 16 Birthday Cake in honor of Phyllis Teller.

Yes, it is Dec. of 1960. We join with the Newirths in having an
Honor Night for Ruth Levine. She is thanked for all her work
in behalf of the Family Circles. It is a gala affair.

Yes, it is still December of 1960. We have a Chanukah Party ,
entertainment and dance at Ave.P and E.15 Street, in Brooklyn.
The kids join us , and we have a wonderful time. Some men have
to leave in the middle to make up a minion (it was a small
synagogue-and not enough men showed up).

Yes, it is Jan. of 1961. Our newly founded teen age groups meet
and go to see"Sparticus".
A motion is passed to send the UJA a contribution.

Yes, it is March 3,1961 . We have an adult Purim Party. We play
Bingo and Herb shows some films. A very pleasant party.

Yes, it is May of 1961. We have a party in Honor of Israel Independence
Day Thirteenth Anniversary. We all get Israel mezzuzzes as gifts,
Our singing is off key, but wonderful to hear. Thanks to Herb, the
Israeli movie is delightful. Just a lovely day.

We had previously planned a bowling match for May 14th. It is now
discovered that, that is Mothers Day. All the Schottenfeld mothers are
outraged that we would rather bowl, than do them honor, so the men
beat a hasty retreat and decide that Oct.29th sounds like a better
day for bowling.

45

Yes, it is June 11,1961. We go to Tess and Sid for a picnic. We
bring food and towels for the pool. We find the grounds rather
soft, as Sid put out a layer of horse manure recently, and covered
it with a thin layer of earth, so the grass would grow. If manure
is the thing that makes grass grow, then, Sid must have the most
fertile land in Freehold. We have a great time.

Yes, it is June 25,1961. We go to Messers. We are in the company
of The Newirth Family Circle, and the Levine Family Circle.
Unfortunately it rains, and a damper is put on all outside activities.
Our softball game with the Newirths is called because of rain.
They claim they could have murdered us, as the best players on
their side were in attendance. We still have a wonderful time.

Yes, it is Aug.20,1961. Today, Faye and Ronnie
Rosenfeld welcome their 3rd child. At his Bris
on Aug.27th, they name him Ira.
*note-on photo Ira (in sailor suit) is flanked by
    grandpa Jack Kessler and Harvey and Carol.

Yes, it is Oct.29,1961. We go to the Cross Bay Bowling Alley for a
competitive Bowling Match. Michael Zudiker comes out with top
honors, Alan Schottenfeld and Hy Zudiker are tied for 2nd, and
Herb Schottenfeld gets 3rd position. All are presented with cups
for their feat.

Yes, it is Nov.5,1961. There is a milk strike in New York. Sid and
Tess are very thoughtful and bring in cases of the stuff from
New Jersey, to distribute to the New York Members.

Yes, it is Dec.of 1961. We have a Chanukah Party for the kids.
The questions are the same, even the wrong answers are the same.
But, what changed is the lolly pops. They used to be round and flat,
now they are all round and thick. But, we have a pleasant day.

Yes, it is January of 1962. A motion is made by Lou, to go on a
skiing trip. It is discussed and keeps getting tabled. Later ,Lou
is to go on his own and comes home with a broken shoulder. He
no more brings it up.

Yes, it is March of 1962. We have a Purim Party for the kids. The
booths are either getting easier or the kids are getting better.
They win so many prizes, shopping bags to carry them home are at a
premium. Ping Pong balls thrown into a goldfish bowl, where you win
goldfish and all, become the best thing to win.

46

Yes, it is April 28, 1962. Carol Povidlo (Bill
and Lil), becomes Mrs. Irving Weiss . Irving is
a Consultant Engineer . They make a delightful
couple and we have a great time at the wedding.

Yes, it is May 5, 1962. We run a Las Vegas Night at the Fraternal
Clubhouse, in the grand Ballroom. We invite the Newirth Family
Circle, The Levine Family Circle and the Levitz Family. We expect
many more, but, 55 people do show. Proceeds , after expenses are to be
donated to Youth Aliya. Everyone has a good time. Lots of food is
left over.
After all proceeds and expenses are tabulated by our auditor, Herb,
we find we had a loss of 20 dollars. We do make a motion at the
next meeting to send Youth Aliya 15 dollars any way. So our net
loss amounts to $40.00. But, we do have fun.

Yes, it is May of 1962. We send a check to the UJA for 25 dollars.
We congratulate Aunt Feiga and Uncle Morris on their 25th Anniversary.
We congratulate Herb on his becoming a partner in the Mizer Law
Firm and a Vice President of United Artists.

Yes, it is June of 1962. 56 Schottenfelds and 55 members of the Levine
Family Circle, meet at Messers , and spend the day together. we have
a wonderful time.

Yes, it is July 22, 1962. We go to Sebago Lake, near Bear Mountain,
for a picnic. It is a fun filled day.

Yes, it is Nov. 4, 1962. A clothes rack is again discussed. On wet
days, the ones whose coats are on the bottom of the pile, have to
go home carrying them, as the ones on top leaked down and the damp
smell is overpowering.

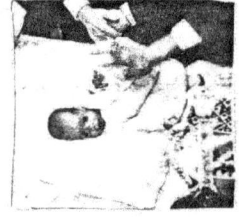

Yes, it is Dec. 6, 1962. Carol and Irving Weiss
become a Mom and Dad . At his Bris, they name
their son, Bruce.

Yes, it is Dec. 8, 1962. A Suprise Party is held at the home of Lil
and Art, in honor of Herb Schottenfeld, in appreciation for all the
work he did and is doing for the Family Circle. He is genuinely
surprised.

47

Yes,it is Dec.30,1962.Ruth Zudiker,Ruth Levine and Lou,run a Chanukah
Party for the Children. The games are delightful.The story of Chanukah
is enjoyed.The children have fun with the dreidels and Chanukah gifts
they receive. Everyone has fun.

Yes,it is Mar.3,1963. Danny makes a recording of the whole meeting
and then plays it back.We are surprised to hear what we always knew.
We are a very noisy group.

Yes,it is March 30,1963. We go to see "Seidman and Sons". We then
go to Ratners as planned. A fun day.

Yes,it is April 21,1963. We meet at the Cross Bay Bowling Alley
for a competitive match. Hy Zudiker gets a Schottenfeld Family Circle
trophy,for having the best score.

Yes,it is May 5,1963. We celebrate Israel Independence Day.We see
an Israeli Film,have a 15th Anniversary of Israel cake,complete
with an Israel Candle Lighting Ceremony.Everyone present gets a
miniature Torah,as a remembrance.
A 25 dollar check is sent to the UJA.

Yes,it is July 28,1963. For a summer outing , Sarah invites the
family circle to her bungalow in Monticello. The date selected
isn't too good,most everyone is busy. Only the Danny Levitz family
is able to attend. They report that they had a good time. Mostly
resting.

Yes,it is Aug.of 1963.We join Tess and Sid
Kornbluh,in celebrating their son Gary's
Bar Mitzvah. It is a great Simcha.

Yes,it is Sept.8,1963. A motion is passed to start saving for
a 25th Family Circle Anniversary to be held in 1967.

Yes,it is Oct.6,1963. We make the last payment to the cemetery for
our cemetery plot.
Frieda and Lou invite everyone to their home,to meet with Col.Lasky
of the Israeli Army,where the topic of conversation will be the
establishment of a new village in Israel,to be funded by Brooklyn
Jewry.
The family circle votes to give $25.00 for the project. Pippa gives
$18.00 Chai for herself. Very lovely.

48

Yes, it is April 11, 1964. She was a girl friend of his kid
sister, who visited each other often. She thought he was adorable.
When she was 12 years old, he would tell her, "Go home squirt, and
take your dolls with you."
When she got to be 14, he would tell her, "Get lost, kid."
When she was 15, he gave her a man to child kiss on the cheek,
and said hewas going into the Air Corp., where he expected to
meet all kinds of women.
She was 18, when he came home, and he couldn't help but notice
how the squirt filled out.
She was 19, when he noticed how the little kid, had grown into
a beautiful, statuesque, young lady and said he wasn't doing anything
that evening, and would she like to go to the movies.
By the time she was 20, he was totally smitten and today,
Diana Kessler becomes Mrs. Joel Rosenblatt.

Yes,it is Oct.12,1963. David Schottenfeld
becomes a Bar Mitzvah.He does his parents
proud when he is called to the Torah. His
reception is a gala affair in Hillel Jewish
Center.

Yes,it is Oct.1963. A 2nd son is born to Isabel and Jerry Povidlo.
At his Brith ,they name him Michael.

Yes,it is Nov.3,1963.At the meeting we are surprised with a visit
from Ethel and Sam Schottenfeld (from the floor covering Schottenfelds).
We have a delightful time with them.
We have a Mortgage Burning Ceremony,and burn a reasonable facsimile,
of our cemetery mortgage. At one point,Danny,who is in charge of
kindling the fire,lets it get away from him,and we almost get to
burn down the Fraternal Clubhouse. Sidney is in charge of the water
pitcher,and gets to cool things down.

Yes,it is Nov.22,1963.A very sad day. Our beloved "Uncle Jake"
suddenly passes away.We are all grieved. He leaves lots of wonderful
memories. He is buried in the Family Circle Plot. Originally,it
was his suggestion that we purchase a family plot,in order that
some day in the future ,we will all be together.

Yes,it is Jan.5,1964. Jack Teller resigns as Editor-in Chief. He
volunteered 3 months before to write a family newspaper,but now finds
it is too big a job. So,he quit before he could get out a single
issue. Lil (Bills) had volunteered to run it off on her mimeo machine,
so she too gets off the hook.
Herb Schottenfeld is elected president-on his campaign promise
to get a coat rack.
An announcement is made that Diana Kessler is engaged to Joel
Rosenblatt.

Yes,it is March 4,1964. We go to see "What makes Sammy run". It
stars Steve Lawrence. We all enjoy.

Yes,it is April 5,1964. We decide not to go to Singers for a Summer
outing,as they want to charge us 6.50 to 7.50 (if you want Steak)
per person,for the day. This is to include 1 brunch and 1 dinner.
It is too much-the nerve of them.

Yes,it is April 11,1964. Today Diana
Kessler becomes Mrs. Joel Rosenblatt.
They make a gorgeous couple at their
reception. It is a wonderful evening.

49

Yes, it is June 26, 1964. It is Steve Schottenfelds
(Frieda and Lou) Bar Mitzvah. He is just great
when reading the portion of the Torah and saying
Mussef. Alan helps by finishing the service with
Ain Kelohanu. His kiddush in Shul is enjoyed.
His reception is very lively.

Yes, it is Nov. 1, 1964. A motion is made that 3 Junior members of the
organization, be advised of everything there is to know about the
cemetery part . Herb suggests we table it for 10 years.

Yes, it is Dec. of 1964. Ruth Levine runs the Chanukah Party and it is
enjoyed by the adults , as well as children.

Yes, it is Jan. 17, 1965. We go to Cafe Sabra. Hannah made the arrangement.
We enjoy the dinner and entertainment. Some couples even get to fit
on the dance floor, and dance.

Yes, it is Feb. 6, 1965. We make a contribution to the UJA of 25 Dollars.
We try to pick a show to go to. Lil (Arts) saw them all, so we decide
on a ballet. It was really a choice between a Opera or a Ballet.
Some choice. .

Yes, it is March of 1965. We have a Purim Party, consisting of kids
dressed up in costume, games for kids and an adult dance contest.
Loads of fun and laughter.

Yes, it is March 27, 1965. We celebrate the sweet 16 of Judy Levitz,
with a party at Art and Lil.

Yes, it is April 16, 1965. Diana and Joel
Rosenblatt become the proud possessors
of their first child. They name their
daughter Cynthia Dawn.

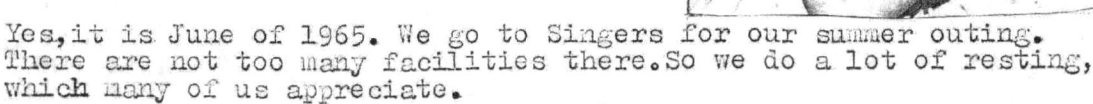

Yes, it is June of 1965. We go to Singers for our summer outing.
There are not too many facilities there. So we do a lot of resting,
which many of us appreciate.

50

Yes,it is still 1965. At the age of 19,
Alan Kornbluh becomes a soldier. He cuts
a handsome figure in uniform.

Yes,it is May 2,1965. We have an Israeli Anniversary Celebration.
The program is enjoyed. We also celebrate the 75th Birthday of
Morris Greifer.

Yes,it is July of 1965. Alan Schwartz,who
isn't aware yet that he is later to marry
Roz Schottenfeld,becomes a Bar Mitzva.

Yes,it is Dec.of 1965. We have a great time at our Chanukah Party.
The format didn't change much-but-is still a lot of fun.

Yes,it is Jan.15,1966. Freddie Levitz becomes
a Bar Mitzvah. Fred is a member of the Choir,
and has a wonderful voice. His Yeshiva training
shows up. His reception is a jumping affair.

Yes,it is Feb.27,1966. We go to see the show"Zulu and the Zeda".
We all enjoy it immensely. We enjoy the after theatre dinner in
addition.

Yes,it is March 3,1966. The kids have a great time at our Purim
Party.The adults have more fun than the kids at the games.

51

Yes, it is March 17,1966. Carol and Irving Weiss
today become parents to a 2nd child. She is a
lovely daughter they name , Michelle.

*note- photo-Michelle poses with brother Bruce.

Yes, it is June 11,1966. Michael Zudiker today marries Mona Russo.
They make a lovely couple. Mona is a welcome addition to the family.

Yes, it is OCTOBER 2 of 1966. Michael Schottenfeld becomes a Bar Mitzva.
It pours that day. As part of the services, the Rabbi makes a prayer for
rain. Herb runs up to the Bema to ask, if the Rabbi can please talk to
G_D , and see if Great Neck could be by-passed that day. At that moment ,
what Herb did not need, was more rain. As it was, the tent that Lorraine
and Herb erected, for the reception, was just about floating away.
Anyway, we have a fabulous time. The band is great, and for the first
time we dance on a floating dance floor. The food is delicious.

Yes, it is Dec.11,1966. We go to Lakewood for the day. Some go on
an exciting Buggy Ride, others go sledding, and still others have
a really tough touch tackle football game. Some plays are real sneaky.

Yes, It is March of 1967. We have a Purim Party that has kids trying
to break balloons by sitting on them. Then we have musical chairs.
You should hear the sqveeching.

Yes, it is June 17,1967. Phyllis Teller today
becomes Mrs. Richard Block. Richard is an ecology
major.

Yes, we will never forget June of 1967. Israel is at war. We are all
concerned. We vote to send our entire treasury, the sum of 250 Dollars,
to the UJA.
We write letters addressed to the President, our Senators, and our
Congressmen, telling them of our concern for Israel, and we expect
them to act accordingly. Lorraine is given the task of mailing them.
Michael Schottenfeld (Lorraine and Herbies), reads a special prayer
for Israel.

Yes, it is July 2,1967. Martin Kornbluh and Natalie Horowitz, become husband and wife today. Marty sets the pace of the day, by doing a Hora
in the aisle going to the Chupa. The rest of the evening is all fun.

52

 Yes,it is Sept.of 1967. Eugene Berger becomes a
Bar Mitzva.His reception is a stomping affair.

Yes,it is Nov.5,1967. We make a decision,that when our meeting room
lease is up in April (we moved uptown when the Fraternal Clubhouse
gave up) ,we would not renew. We would go back to meeting in members
homes.

Yes,it is Dec.13,1967. A 2nd child is born
to Diana and Joel Rosenblatt. He shows
promise of being a soccer player,before he is
born,by kicking like mad. At his Brith,his
parents name him Jack. They also, right then and
there ,decide,that his Bar Mitzvah will be
on Dec.7,1980.

Yes,it is Dec.30,1967. Lorraine,as Program Chairman ,invites all
teen agers to a meeting at her home.

Yes,it is Jan.7,1968. A tragedy again strikes the family circle.
We mourn the passing away of our darling "Tante Feiga". She left
so many fond memories,she will never be forgotten. Her vivacious-
ness,her warmth, her greetings,her total disregard for her own
ills in being concerned with others,is implanted in the minds of
all who were privileged to know her.
We convey our regrets to Uncle Morris Greifer,and the children.

Yes,it is Jan.21,1968. Today Ronnie Zudiker became Mrs.Richard
Zusman. Ronnie is a gorgeous gal. They make a lovely couple.

Yes,it is Feb.4,1968.Lorraine makes a report that as a result of
the meeting in her homeof the Young Teen Agers and Young married
couples,a new meeting is sheduled at the home of Mona and Michael
Zudiker.Judy Levitz and Roz Schottenfeld,feel,that as singles,
they lack common ground with the married couples.But,all are
willing to try.
We congratulate Phyllis on her getting her masters.

Yes, it is March 3,1968.We have a book discussion on "Everything but
Money",by Sam Levinson. Lorraine is the moderator,and does a
wonderful job. Everyone enjoys.

Yes,it is March of 1968.We have a Purim Party,run by Frieda and
Lorraine,and assisted by Michael Zudiker,Natalie Kornbluh and
Harvey Rosenfeld. They do an outstanding job. The kids love it.
.Toys are distributed. Everyone has a good time.

53

RUTH L.   HANNAH   RUTH Z.

RUTH   HY

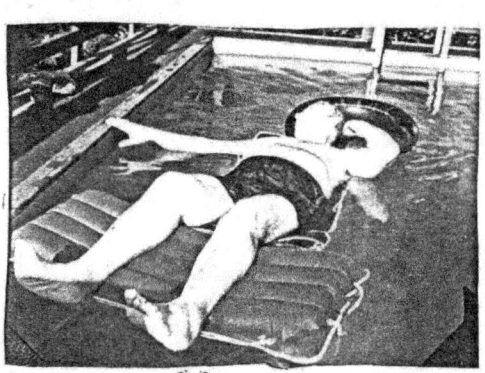

SID

Yes,it is July of 1968.We go to
the Kornbluh home in Freehold, for
the day. Tess and Sid are delightful
hosts. We have a picnic,barbecue,
and go swimming in the pool.
Some members can't make it and miss
a great day.

Yes,it is Oct.27,1968.Ruth Levine is delegated to go to our former
meeting place in Yorkville,and pickup the stuff we left there.
She reports,not only did she not find our stuff- - she couldn't
find the locker we put our stuff into.

Yes,it is Nov.24,1968. Today Naomi Schottenfeld
becomes Mrs.David Kudish. It is a wonderful,
happy reception.

Yes,it is Dec.of1968. Harvey Rosenfeld
becomes a Bar Mitzva.

*note- photo- he poses with sister Carol
          and brother Ira.

54

Yes,it is Dec.of 1968. We have a gala Chanukah Party,and rent a room
at the Avenue Z Jewish Center for the occasion.Everything is planned
except the heavy snow.In spite of it ,we have a large crowd.
Entertainers were hired,who organize group dances and games.Lorraine
takes care of all the planning,and did a great job. We all had fun.

Yes,it is Feb.3,1969.Our scheduled meeting is at Lorraine and Herbs
home.For an after dinner treat,we are to see a film.
A problem develops ,Herbs projector breaks down. Suddenly,we have
more projector experts than anything else. Danny asks for a screw
driver,Sonny would like a hammer, Lou says he works best with a pair
of pliers,Sid Kornbluh says if Herb had a stillson wrench,he could
probably fix it,Hy Zudiker wants to know when someone will get away
and let him get near the machine, and Nat Levine wants to know
whether a projector is like a hand bag. Herb justs stands by sweating,
and thinking his projector will never be the same.
Well anyway,nothing helps,we never get it to work.

Yes,it is March of 1969.We run an Adult and Childrens Party. Everyone
plays games.

Yes,it is April 13,1969. We are delighted at the request of Bessie
Schottenfeld (Widow of Arthur-Uncle Willies),that she would like
to join the Schottenfeld Family Circle.She is the only member of
the Uncle Willie Family,to become a member.

Yes,it is May 8,1969.Today Barry Levine and
Gail Kraf,are married.It is a lovely affair.

Yes,it is May 18,1969. Steve (Lorraine and Herb) Schottenfeld,becomes
a Bar Mitzva. It is a sunny,delighful day. The tent is festive.
The band is great. The food is excellent. We dance in the gentle
breezes that filter through the tent. Just a lovely , unforgettable
day.

Yes,it is Oct 20,1969. A first child is born
to Phyllis and Richard Block. They name their
daughter,Sharon Amy.

55

Yes,it is Nov.23,1969. We enjoy discussing the book "The Chosen",
so much,that we agree to continue discussing it at the next meeting.

Yes,it is Dec.of 1969. We go to the Homowack Lodge. The food is
excellent. Outdoor activities are great. Indoors (for those who
prefer Florida weather)is just wonderful. At 3 PM,it starts to snow.
Just little drops that aren't even sticking.
We are advised that if you are leaving for home today,to go now.
We laugh,how much snow could fall in an hour.
We find out. By 4 o'clock,we can't find our cars ,Completely buried.
A tractor has to pull you out,once you find your car. We are also to
learn other things,if you are going in the wrong direction-just
keep going —don't turn around (You never make it). If you run
off the road,Just watch out for the cows,but don't stop.
We don't know how,but everyone manages to get home.

Yes,it is Feb 1,1970. We go to see "Melody Lingers On", and have a
good time. We also went to eat,but we know not where.

Yes,it is March of 1970.We have a Purim Party at Lorraine and Herbs
home. Some members and their children go ice skating,others just
ate and ate until it was time to see a movie in Herbs Projection
Room.
Herb wanted to make sure we see the film,so he borrowed a neighbors
projector.
Well , the thing didn't work.
Danny ,Lou and Hy were willing to take the projector apart to fix it,
but Herb shied away from the suggestion. So we all went back to eating.

Yes,it is April of 1970. Eric Schottenfeld
becomes a Bar Mitzva. The reception is a
lively affair. Lots of stomping.

Yes,it is May 3,1970.We see the slides Frieda and Lou took of their
visit to Israel.They must have taken shots of every tree there,as the
showing takes many hours. They hold the interest of everyone.

Yes,it is June of 1970.We have a picnic at Tess and Sid Kornbluh.
Loads of fun and then came the rain. We all duck indoors. The
women waste no time , and do shopping instead of picnicing.

Yes,it is June 14,1970. We hold our first Schottenfeld Family Circle
Cemetery Memorial Service.The services are dignified and become an
annual event. Lorraine and Herb are in charge,send out the notices,
assign different people to conduct the service, select the prayers ,
zerox copies for everyone and set the format for the future annual
services. They also supply a kiddush at the cemetery grounds after
the service.

56

Yes,it is Aug,29,1970 . Sheryl Levine,today becomes
Mrs. Marc Graber. They make a lovely couple.

Yes,it is Aug.30,1970. Roz Schottenfeld today
becomes Mrs.Alan Schwartz. They are a
delightfull couple. The reception is just
grand.

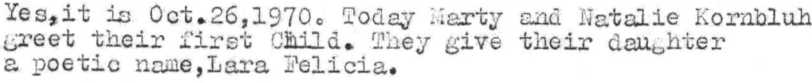

Yes,it is Sept.12,1970. Barry and Gail
Levine welcome their first child.
At his Bris,they name their son, Steven.

*note-photo- Steve poses with sister
             Suzanne.

Yes,it is Oct.26,1970. Today Marty and Natalie Kornbluh
greet their first Child. They give their daughter
a poetic name,Lara Felicia.

Yes,it is Nov.1,1970 . We review the book "Portnoy's Complaint".
It is discovered that those who argue the most, are those who never
read the book. The consensus of opinion is ,its not as great as
they say it is,

Yes,it is Jan.of 1971. We go to see"The Story Theatre". Tickets
were arranged for by Lorraine. We then go to Siegels for.dinner.
Hannah does all the arranging for that. Both parts are enjoyed.

Yes,it is Feb.15,1971. Today Sheryl and Marc
Graber,welcome their first child. They call
their daughter Shawn
* note-photo- Shawn kissing brother Ethan.

57

Yes,it is March of 1971. We have a Purim Party for all,at Lorraine
and Herb.The older play Touch Football, the younger play basketball,
and the youngest get to hear the Story of Purim,play carnival games
and win prizes.
Herb shows a narrative film,Leonard Bernstein,"Journey to Jerusalem".
It is delightfully enjoyed by those of all ages. Herb's projector
works right to the end.

Yes,it is April 25,1971. We vote to send the UJA our annual donation.

Yes,it is June 20,1971. We go to Goldmans in West Orange,New Jersey.
Everything adds up to a good time. The weather is good,getting there
is easy,the food is good and the facilities are great.

Yes,it is July 20,1971. Tragedy again strikes the family. Beloved
Pippa passes away. She will be remembered by all. She was always
concerned about the whole family.
We wonder how she did it. She had 7 children to feed , clothe,bathe
and send to school.She stayed up with them a whole night,to comfort
them when they had their childhood diseases. She got up at 5 AM with
Isaac,to give him breakfast before he left for work.She then stoked
the coal furnace and took out the ashes.She cleaned the large house
with no outside help (it was always spotless).She was always ready
with lunches and dinners.She would feed upwards of 50 people ,friends
and relatives,who came to visit on weekends,without a murmur, and
thanked everyonefor coming to see her. Weekdays,the 7 kids and their
friends (20 or 30 strong),would gather for singing sessions or just
playing instruments as loud as they could. She would smile and hand
out refreshments. She would make a drink from Roses we grew in the
yard (by boiling the petals),that was delicious.She would watch the
grape vines,as to when we should remove the grapes to make passover
wine.She would feed the animals(goats,chickens,dogs and crazy pets we
had,like white rats.She would go shopping and flick her own chickens.
She would prepare for the holidays and the Sabbath.She would go to
the synagogue and then come home andfind time to read Rashi or the
Talmud. Her best pleasure,was to read Bintele Brief and cry like
mad.She was always cheerful and sat down with the kids to talk things
out.If that didn't work-you got a' cat of nine tails'across your bottom.
Yes,how did she do it.

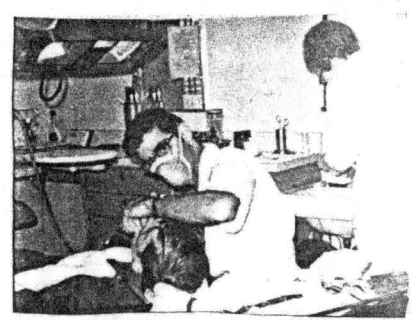

Yes,it is Aug.of 1971. Alan Schottenfeld
becomes a member of the U.S.Army Dental
Corp. He is to see service in Kentucky
and then Korea. He gets his discharge
in Aug.of 1973.

    *note-photo- that's Nurse
     Margaret Forman
     We wonder whether the soldier
     patient knows that Alan just
     got out of Dental School.

Yes,it is Sept26,1971.At the meeting,Lou makes a report that the
30th Anniversary Committee,ofwhich he is a member,is formulating
plans,and that every one is in for a great surprise.The members
think that he will be part of those who are surprised as they do
not believe that . either he or Lorraine ever met to plan anything
for the 30th Anniversary. The nerve.

Yes,it is Sept.of 1971. Art and Lil move to Florida,to start a
different phase of their life.

                    FR

Yes, it is Oct.10,1971. Matthew Schottenfeld today becomes a Bar Mitzva.
We are invited to a lovely Synagogue Service and a lawn tent reception.
It not only rains today-it has been pouring for 3 days. Lorraine and
Herb, think of renting rowboats so we can get past the entrance, but,
we have the greatest time.

Yes, it is Dec.26,1971. Today David Schottenfeld
married Ann Wasserman. They are to live in Florida.
The wedding reception is delightful.

Yes, it is the meeting of Jan.9,1972. We discuss the book "The Tenants".
Lorraine does her usual great job as moderator. It is split 50/50
as to those who enjoy the book and those who would rather have watched
the late,late show,instead of reading it.

Yes, it is Feb.27,1972. Lorraine and Herb again volunteer their
home as a setting for a Purim Party. The party is a great success,
and the host and hostess are just marvelous.

Yes, it is Feb.28,1972. Naomi and David Kudish
become parents today. They name their first
child, a daughter , Lisa Faith.

Yes, it is March 12,1972.We go to see the unforgettable,"Fiddler on
the Roof". Lorraine arranged for the tickets,which was quite a
feat. Sarah arranged for the luncheon at Lou Siegels. We get a
special section for ourselves. We also feel at home,because we
have to put our coats piled up on chairs , and they keep falling
off.

Yes, it is April 2,1972.We have our
first 3rd Seder. Danny,Hannah,Herb,
Lorraine and all the food servers
knock themselves out.It is held in
Frieda and Lou's downstairs apartment.
The place is jammed. In fact,if you
had an inside seat,that was it. You just
didn't go to the bathroom.If you
screamed you just had to-you had to
prove extreme emergency-26 people had
to move.
Anyway,every one enjoyed.

MICHAEL SONNY CAROL RUTH JACK PHYLLIS
FAITH ELAYNE
CIANTA(ANN)

59

HANNAH   DANNY

3RD
SEDER
APR.
2
1972

JACK   RUTH

RUTH + NAT
LEVINE

RUTH + HY
ZUDIKER

RUTH   ANITA
KESSLER   MRS BALTER

JUDY   FAY   HANNAH

DIANA   ILENE   JACKIE   JOEL
CINDY

60

LIL   ART   TEDDY   SARAH

MATTHEW STEVE HERB HOWARD

3rd Seder
Apr, 2,1972

RUTH JACK PHYLLIS SHARON

Yes,it is April 1972. We mourn the passing away of Bessie Schottenfeld.
Bessie was our only link to the Uncle Willie side of the family. She
was the widow of Unle Willies oldest son, Arthur.

Yes,it is the meeting of May 7th 1972. We have a debate on many topics
of interest,prepared by Lorraine. You are assigned the topic and the
side you will debate. It is greatly enjoyed.

Yes,it is May 28,1972.We have a memorial service at the cemetery.
Traffic is heavy and many arrive late. We learn never to pick a
date that is a holiday week end. We get services underway about
an hour late.

Yes,it is June 25,1972.We saved and
saved and the day finally arrived,
for our 30th Anniversary Yacht trip
and ceremony.
Herb and Lorraine make all arrangments,
and the day consists of a yacht trip
that stops at Nyack,where we board
waiting cabs that take us to the Nyack
Hotel for Dinner. Then back to the Yacht.
The only thing that was not planned, was
the rain. It rained so hard,that,
visibility was zero.
But, G_D had compassion for his people,
and when we get underway,the sun comes
out,a true miracle.
On board we have a cocktail party,and
play games. At the hotel,we have speeches
and a presentation is made to honor
Lorraine and Herb for their efforts
in behalf of the organization.
Everyone receives a cup and saucer which are engraved,as a momento
of the occasion.
The entire population of Nyack turns out to see us disembark and
embark.The dinner is delicious. We have out own band on board and
at the dinner. We have a dance contest.An unforgettable day.

61

30TH
ANN.
YACHT
TRIP

SARAH - RUTH - HY - RUTH - HANNAH

RUTH - JACK

SID
HARRY
FRIEDA
LIL

ELAINE - FRIEDA - SONNY - RUTH

HY - HANNAH

62

TED   SARAH

LORRAINA   HY   FLORRIE
SHIRLEY

30TH

ANN

YACHT

TRIP

LOU   SARAH   BILL   HANNAY   RUTH
HARRY

HARRY   TESS   RUTH   JACK   HAROLD
FLORRIE

SID   FRIEND   HANNAH

Yes , it is Oct 8,1972. The UJA sends a letter asking for funds which
are needed. we vote to send them a check.

Yes,it is Oct.11,1972. Ronnie and Richard Zusman
welcome a 1st child. At his Brith, they name their
son,Eric.

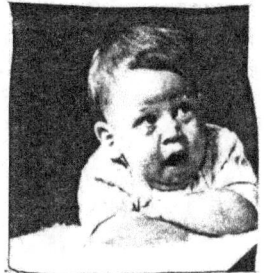

'63

Yes,it is Nov.12,1972. We see the first half of a delightful film
on the development of the State of Israel,compliments of Herb.
The 2nd half has to be cancelled because of mechanical difficulties
of Herbies projector. The part we see,is just great.

Yes,it is Dec.3rd 1972. We go to see the show,"The Proposition".
For dinner. arrangements are made at Lou Siegel. It is a most
enjoyable day. The show is good and the food is good.

Yes,it is Feb.4,1973. We start saving for a family circle meeting
to be held at the "Western Wall",in Jerusalem,on our 35th Anniversary.
We save and save,but unfortunately,we never make the trip together,
as it is too much to expect ,that everyone will be able to go to
Israel at the same time.
We discuss the book "My Name Is Asher Lev" by Potok. Everyone
enjoyed reading the book and a highly animated discussion greeted
Lorraine,who was the moderator.

Yes,it is April 22,1973.Today ,Howard Schottenfeld becomes a Bar
Mitzva.All week long ,everyone including Herb and Lorraine has
been listening to weather reports and forecasts. If someone predicts
rain for Sunday-you heard a groan.
However,the day turns out just beautiful. The Services are delightful.
The Tent is heated and lovely. We all have a wonderful time.

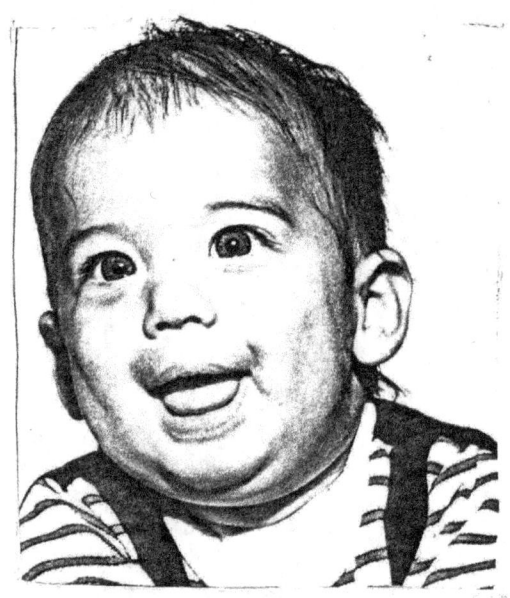

Yes,it is May 25,1973. Natalie
and Martin Kornbluh welcome
their 2nd child. At his Brith,
he is named Alec Geoffrey.

Yes,it is June 24,1973. We have a Memorial Service at the Cemetery.
Herb and Danny lead the family in the Services. There is a Kiddush,
which follows.

64

Yes, it is Sept. 6, 1973. Gail and
Barry Levine have their 2nd child.
They name her Suzanne.

* note-photo- Suzanne poses with
  brother Steven.

Yes, it is Sept. 9, 1973. A delightful
combination Picnic and meeting is
held at Diana and Joel Rosenblatt.
The host and hostess are just
lovely. The weather is great and
their home is beautiful.

LOOK WHO IS HERE! NO HISTORY TEST

ALAN   JUDY FAYE LISA ROZ

FAYE LISA ROZ CAROL FAY

NAOMI SUSAN SARAH FLORENCE

DIANA JOEL NAOMI GREETING FLOR.

65

BILL JACK DAN

Yes, it is Sept.15,1973. Phyllis and
Richard Block, today become the
proud parents of a 2nd daughter.
They name her Ellen Michelle.

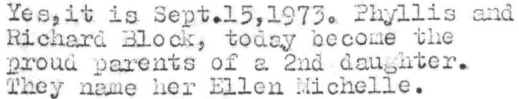

66

Yes,it is Oct.7,1973. We come prepared to celebrate the 25th Anniversary,
of Lorraine and Herb,but have to postpone it,because the guests of
honor cannot come to the meeting. We decide to incorporate the anniversary with our Chanukah party on Dec.2nd.
We vote to send the UJA 100 Dollars for the Emergency Fund.

Yes,it is Dec.2,1973. We have a 25th Anniversary Celebration of
Lorraine and Herb,and also a Chanukah Party. We are so busy today,
we even start on time.
First,our cake lighting ceremony (we do not know whether we are using
the same cake that was made the month before),we let Herb and Lorraine
taste the first piece,just to make sure.
We then play Schottenfeld Bingo for prizes. Then have a big poker
game for pennies. Then see a film "I came from Jerusalem",courtesy
of Herb. We have a very busy but delightful day.

Yes,it is Jan.1974. We have a meeting at Ruth and Nat Levine. Herb
brings his new wide lens that attaches to his new delayed action
camera. We get to test it. We all gather around, Herb sets the camera,
runs around the kitchen to get into the back of the picture and
it works.

Yes,it is March 3,1974. We celebrate Purim,but this year is different
from all other years. Instead of the children supplying the entertainment for the adults, the children are to sit,and watch the adults
enact the story of Purim.
We rent the ballroom of the Ave.Z Jewish Center.Parts are given out,
actors have to make their own costumes. Michael is to enact his part
on crutches,as he has broken a leg.
Sonny ,who plays the part of Haman, is so hated by the kids,he is
booed and has to guard against getting spit at.
We also celebrate the 50th birthday of Herb. Lorraine gets to pop
out of a cake.
We have the greatest of times. Everyone plays their part well.
Cameras and flashbulbs keep popping.Just like a professional show.
An unforgettable day.

67

68

HY   JACK   Bill

69

CINDY ROSENBLATT   70

Yes,it is April 21,1974.We go to see "That Championship Season".
For dinner,we go to Moshe Peking,for a kosher Chinese meal.

Yes, it is May 5, 1974. We vote to send the UJA
a check for 25 Dollars. Michael Schottenfeld
leaves for Israel to live on a Kibbutz in the
West Bank. He is to become a member of the
Israeli Air Force and then a member of a "Gush
Emunim" Kibbutz in the Sinai. He is the only
member of our organization to seek Aliya, until
now. His 2 visits to us are greatly enjoyed,
and we are all very proud of Michael. Some of
our members visit with him when they go to Israel.
Michael is also the cause of his parents spending
vacations working on Kibbutzim, or taking part in
an archeology dig, which they enjoy so much.
Sonny cannot attend this meeting as he has a broken toe.
It seems he was wearing 2 right shoes, and one toe did
not know where the other toe was going, so they hit.
We see slides of our Purim Show and it is great fun.

Yes,it is June 2,1974. We have a treat in store for us today. Herb
shows us the film "Kazablan". We all enjoy it tremendously.

Yes,it is Aug.10,1974. Stephanie Diamond marries Ronnie Horvitz.
We are to sleep over in Poughkeepsie,and join for breakfast.

Yes,it is Aug.16,1974. Mona and Michael
have a baby son. At his Brith they name
him Steven. He is gorgeous.

Yes,it is Aug.of 1974. Tragedy strikes. Gertrude Schottenfeld
suddenly passes away. Her sister,Mildred ,with whom she **lived,**
is grief stricken. Gert was jst getting over a cataract operation.
it is a blow to the family.

Yes,it is Sept.1,1974.We have a Memorial Service at the Cemetery.
Everyone gets there on time,and we start early. It is a dignified
service. A Kiddush follows.

71

Yes, it is Sept.1974. Ira Rosenfeld today
becomes a Bar Mitzva. The reception is
a lovely affair.

Yes, it is Oct.13,1974. A letter is received from Michael Schottenfeld
in Israel. He sends his love and regards to all of us. He also tells
us of his life in Israel.It is full of hope.

Yes, it is November of 1974. Tragedy again strikes the family. Mildred
Schottenfeld passes away. We are all grief stricken. She was still
grieving for her sister Gertrude. We will never forget her sweetness,
and her kindness.

Yes, it is Dec.15,1974. We go to the Homowach Lodge,for an outing
and a Chanukah Party.We enjoy the facilities and then are given a
room for our party.We tell the story of Chanukah and give out
lots of lollypops to the kids for correct answers.

Yes, it is Jan.of 1975. We go to see the show "Candide". The seats are
not very comfortable,but the show is enjoyed. Those with bad backs ,
walk with their noses scraping the ground. It takes weeks to get our
backs in working order. We have dinner at "Moshe Peking".

Yes, it is Jan 23 1975. Today a son
is born to Sherri and Mark Graber.
He is their 2nd child. At his Brith
they name him Ethan Garrett.

72

Yes,it is Feb.2,1975. At the meeting we play charades,that have been originated by Sonny Schottenfeld. We have a hilarious time.

Yes,it is Feb.23,1975. We have a delightful Purim Party. The songs are sung with much gusto, rather then with artistic abilities. It is much more fun that way.

Yes,it is March 30,1975. We have a 3rd Seder , at Beth El Synagogue. The committee that takes care of running the seder and those that take care of the food and serving,do a great job. We have a great time. Herb tapes the Seder,and we all get to say a few words into his mike,as Herb is to send the tape to Michael in Israel. Michael enjoys it and sends us a lovely Thank You note.

Yes,it is May of 1975. We note that in times of an emergency or a tragedy in the family,there is a lack of communication. Families that are in distress,cannot call everyone. Frieda is elected,to act as central agent. from now on ,if a need arises where everyone has to be notified about something, the family has just to make one call,to Frieda, who will be provided with a listing ,and will do all the calling. Subsequently ,this works very well and Frieda does an excellent job of alleviating,that problem.
We vote to send 25dollars to the UJA.
Starting in September,Ruth Zudiker,is to take the place of Lorraine as Program Chairman,and give Lorraine a much needed rest from that most important but immense job.
Lorrains work for the many years,was the mainstay of the organization. She did it with great zeal and originality. We will miss her.
We wish loads of luck to Ruth Zudiker and thank her for undertaking this laborious job.
We see slides of our 3rd Seder and enjoy.

Yes, it is Oct.5th 1975. We have a Memorial Service at our Cemetery Plot. The Services and prayers are dignified. A Kiddush follows.

Yes,it is Nov.1,1975. Alan Schottenfeld (Frieda and Lou),had gone on a vacation trip to Puerto Rico. There he met Aileene Shuster. The chance meeting,results in their marriage today. It is a lovely reception.

73

Yes,it is Nov.15,1975.
Bruce Weiss today becomes
a Bar Mitzva.
We are all proud of him,
when he reads the portion
of the Torah.He does it so
well. His reception is
just beautiful.
*note-photo-he poses
   today with Grandpa,
   Grandma and sister
   Michelle.

Yes,it is Dec.21,1975. Judy Levitz today becomes
Mrs.Ronnie Karp. Ronnie works for an accountant
office. They make a lovely couple. They find a
nice apartment on Bedford Ave.
Their reception is a lively affair.

Yes,it is Dec.of 1975. We rent a room at the Avenue Z Jewish Center
for our Chanukah Party. We have a great time and the children love
it. They go home with dreidels and prizes.

Yes,it is Jan.4,1976. We welcome Faye and Mac Schottenfeld at the
meeting. Mac,is the son of Avram Shea. It is pleasant to be with
them.

Yes,it is Jan.6,1976. A baby brother is born to
Lisa Kudish. Naomi and David name him Seth,at his
Brith.

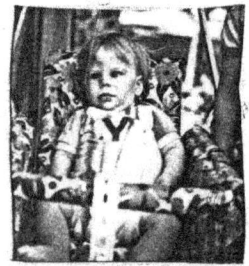

Yes,it is Feb.1,1976. We have a book discussion on "The Other Side
of Midnight". Lou comes to the meeting late and it is in the middle
of the discussion. He thought "Exodus" was the book under discussion,
so without asking,he goes into a 15 minute monologue ,on the book.
He can't figure out why no one seems to know what he's talking about.
Only then was it established that he had the wrong book.

Yes,it is March 7,1976. We go to see the show "Yentle". Most agree
that the acting is great,but,the show is terrible.
We are supposed to go to the "Macabean" for dinner, but after a fast
discussian, it is decided to go to some restaurant on 39thStreet and
9th Ave.

74

Yes,it is April 3,1976. Tragedy again strikes the family. Jack Teller
suddenly passes away. The family is saddened. We are to miss his
presence at the meetings. We share Ruths grief.

Yes,it is April 23,1976. A 2nd child is
born to Ronnie and Richard Zusman. The
latest addition to the family is named
Felicia Elizabeth,by their parents.

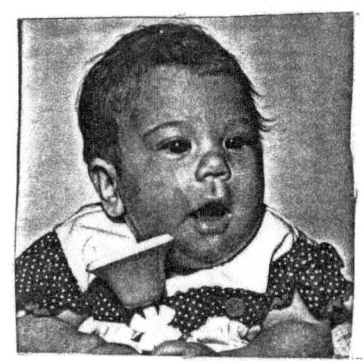

Yes,it is June of 1976. Gary Kornbluh
enlists in the United States Navy.
He is to go to school and become a
communication technition.

Yes,it is June 6,1976. Shirley and Harold Diamond invite us to
a picnic on their lawn,in Poughkeepsee. We have a wonderful time.
The shtarkers hit and catch a softball. If the ball goes over the
fence, you have to get over when the neibors dog isn't looking,or
you are minus 1 pants leg. The hammock is delightful,and the women
gab. We have to make a run for Shirleys' living room when the rains
come. It is a great day.

HAROLD HY DANNY FLOPENCE E LAYNE TESS HANNAH GRIEDA

75

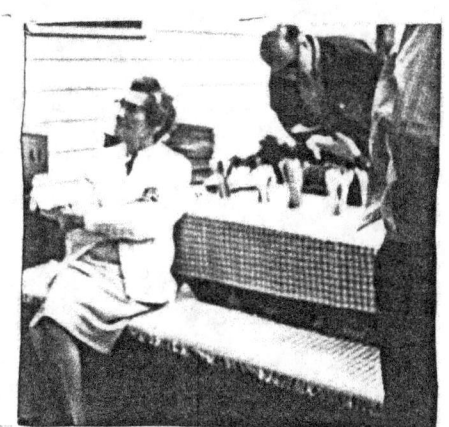

TANTA FANNIE   HAROLD

Yes,we are still picnicing,at
Shirley and Harolds'.

Yes,it is Aug.22,1976. Steve Schottenfeld (Frieda and Lou),is today
married to Joni Florek. It is a
beautiful wedding. The Chupa is
outdoors. The parents of Joni come
in from Israel for the wedding.

Yes,it is Sept.12,1976. We have our annual Memorial Services at the
Family Circle Plot. We also note that the grounds are well kept.
Perhaps it is because Herb and Lorraine,make sure they deliver a
bottle to the keepers at Christmas Time. A Kiddush follows.

Yes,it is Sept.1976. A terrible tradgedy. Beautiful Bonnie Povidlo,
granddaughter of Lil and Bill,passes away. We are all shaken.

76

Yes,it is Oct.of 1976. Uncle Morris Greifer,who lived the last few
years in a Long Beach Senior Citizen Hotel,passes away. We are
saddened by the tragedy.He leaves so many good memories. Who can
also forget the constant cigars he smoked that would go side to
side in his mouth. You could always tell his mood. If the cigar
moved slowly side to side,he was calm. However,if his cigar moved
fast,something was bothering him,and he was annoyed and nervous.
At a poker game ,it was a give away. If his cigar went rapidly from
one side to the other,you had best get out,he had afull house.
Yes,it was always a delight to talk to Uncle Morris.

Yes,it is Oct.18,1976. Today Alan Kornbluh is married to Charlene.
The wedding takes place at her home ,in a western state. It is
too far for all of us to attend,but the close family attends.
Alan and Charlene make their home in Florida.

Yes,it is Oct.1976. Michael Povidlo becomes a Bar Mitzva . Bill and
Lil go to Florida for the Bar Mitzva.

Yes,it is Nov.5,1976. A motion is made and passed that we send a check
for 25 dollars to the UJA.

Yes,it is Dec.1976. Lorraine and Herb are the host and hostess at
our annual Chanukah Party ,which is today held at their home. It
is a lovely day and well attended.

Yes,it is March 6,1977.We go the Cafe Baba for a lovely meal and
an excellent show.It is fun dancing on a dance floor that is 5 feet
by 5 feet,and meant for 3 couples. Instead 30 people pack onto it.
If you don't hold your partner close, you are sure to find yourself
dancing with a stranger. But,we do have a great time.

Yes,it is March 27,1977. We hold our 3rd Seder at Elayne and Sonny.
We are surprised with a visit from Israel of Michael Schottenfeld.
It is a delight to see him.He is Guest of Honor,and we all love him.
The committee does its usual great job of preparing and serving the
food.

Yes,it is June 29,1977. Today Carol Rosenfeld
marries Ted Trachtenberg. Their wedding is
lovely. They settle down in Far Rockaway. Ted
is an accountant.

77

Yes, it is July 27, 1977. Ann and David Schottenfeld
in Florida, are blessed with a lovely baby boy.
They name him Jason Ira at his Brith.

Yes, it is Aug. of 1977. An original copy of our 13th Anniversary
Journal, assembled by Herb and Lorraine Schottenfeld, is found.
Ronnie Karp volunteers to make copies for everyone. Lou mails
them out, and all members enjoy getting them.

Yes, it is Oct. 2, 1977. Even though our treasury is very shaky, and
at a point of being totally obliterated, we vote to send a check
for 25 dollars to the UJA.

Yes, it is Oct. of 1977. We have our annual Memorial Service at the
Cemetery. The Services are conducted with much respect, and show
the love we had for our dear departed.
A Kiddush follows.

Yes, it is Nov. of 1977. Mac and Faye Schottenfeld tell us they are
making a permanent move to a Florida condominian.

Yes, it is Dec. of 1977. Sid Schottenfeld writes a comedy, produces
and directs the play at our Chanukah Party. It is held at Lil and
Bills house.
The songs are terrific and really funny (not like his usual jokes).
It is enacted by the members. We are to have the greatest of times.

78

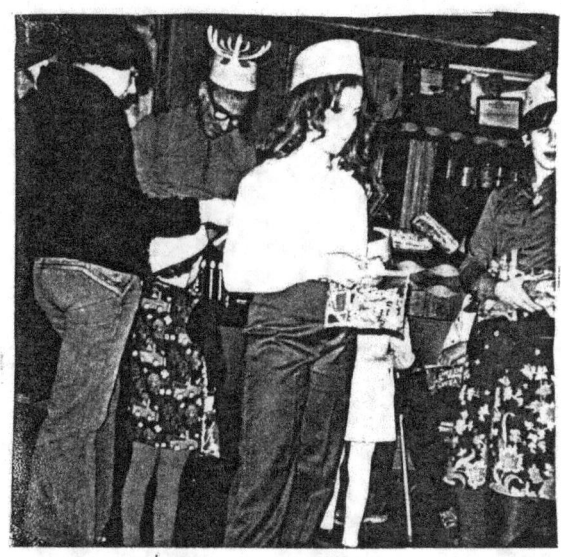

LOU   MICHELLE   CINDY

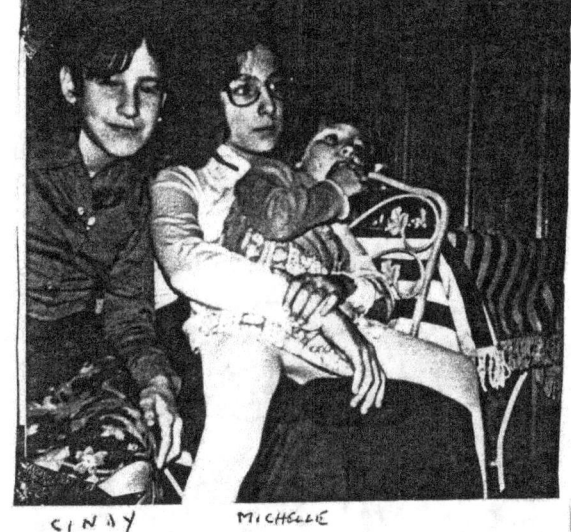

CINDY   MICHELLE

ELLEN ELAYNE CAROL   HANNAH   FAYE

FAYE   HANNAH DIANA RUTH FAY JACK

Yes, it is Jan.8,1978. A discussion of length is held on the question,
"Can Sadat be Trusted". Included in the discussion is , "What will
the decision be about the West Bank". The discussion leads to just
one end. Only time will tell.

Yes, it is March 5,1978. We welcome visitors to our Purim meeting.
It is delightful to see Sid and Evelyn Semel, Fannie Tannenbaum,
George and Adele (Adele is Avram Sheas daughter), Allen Itkowits,
and of coarse always nice to see Ellen (Sonny and Elayne).
We have added a new planned discussion period. Today we discuss
Onkelos, a Roman convert to Judaism, who became a champion of Jews,
and whose interpretation of the Bible is studied to this day.

Yes, it is April 9,1978. We hold our 3rd Seder , at Elayne and Sonny.
The committee consisting of Sonny, Elayne, Hannah , Danny, Ruth Z and
Hy, are commended for their hard work in making this day a successful
one in Schottenfeld Family Circle history of events.

79

Yes,it is June 7,1973. We go to
Shirley and Harold Diamond for
an outing and picnic,on their
lawn.
The day is beautiful,and the
host and hostess are just like
the weather.

RUTHZ   TESS

LIL DAN NAT ELAYNE FRIEDA HANNAH

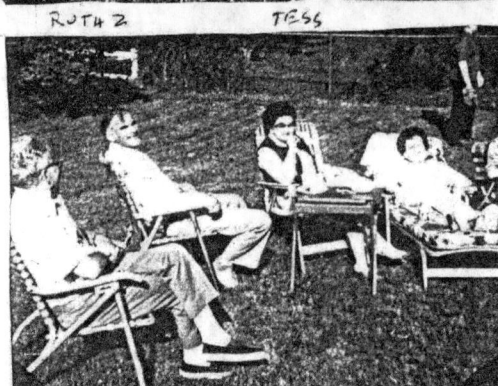

BILL   HARRY   FLORRIE   LIL

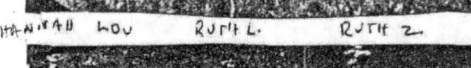

HANNAH LOU   RUTH L.   RUTH Z.

ELAYNE   TANTH GANNY   MRS DALTER

FRIEDA   HANNAH SONNY   RUTH

ELAYNE FRIEDA DANNY

Yes,it is Feb.18,1979. A first
child is born to Aileene and
Alan Schottenfeld,at the Wilkes
Barre General Hospital,in Penn.
She is named Lee.
The Frieda and Louis household
is never to be the same again.

note-photo- A new mother looks
          at her just born daughter.

Lee requests that you pronounce
Wilkes-Barre correctly.
To a native of Wilkes-Barre,it
is pronounced as Wilkes Bahr
(with the Bahr as the same sound
as the first 4 letters of Barren)

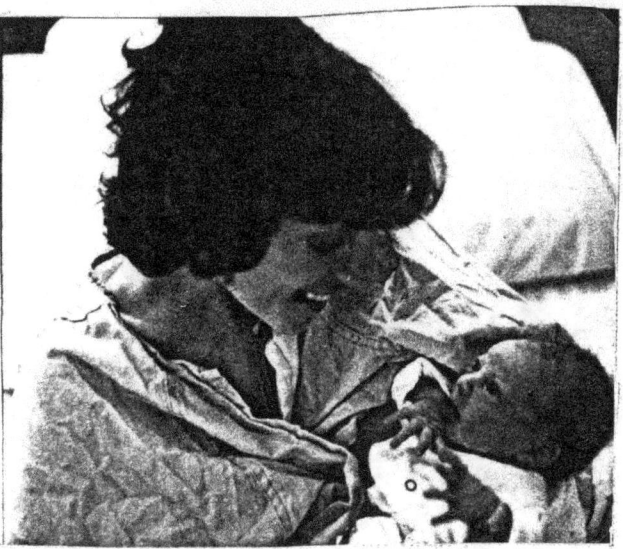

Yes,it is March 8,1979. Today Harvey Rosenfeld
marries Pamela Waxman. Their reception is very
lovely.

Yes,it is March 14,1979. We go to the Cafe Baba,for a Purim Celebration.
The food is good and the entertainment is excellent. Everyone has
a great time.

Yes,it is April of 1979. We have a 3rd Seder and are invited to
hold it at Elayne and Sonny.The committees do an excellent job,
and everyone enjoys.

Yes,it is April 22,1979. Judy and Ronnie Karp
become parents of a first child. They name
their daughter, Alana.

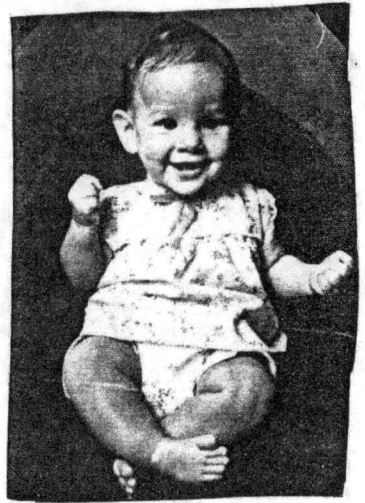

Yes,it is June 10,1979. We go to Shirley and Harold,for an outing
and picnic. The weather is just great. We all have loads of fun.

82

Yes,it is Sept.2,1979. We have Memorial Services at the Cemetery.
Near the end of the Services,a torrential rain hits us very suddenly.
It came down in buckets,in exactly 1 second,from being just cloudy.
Everyone runs for their cars,except Ruth Zudiker,Lou and Danny. They
stand their ground,throughout the downpour,oblivious of getting
drenched, and finish the services-right to the last word.
Now,that's dedication.

Yes,it is Dec.2,1979. We have a sur-
prise (to Lou- everyone else knew
about) Chanukah Party. Lou is honored
by the Schottenfeld Family Circle..
It comes complete with throwing
lolly pops at him,whether or not he
knew the answers to the questions
asked by Herb. He is then presented
with 2 blowup pictures, the back of one
is signed by everyone present,who also
write lovely things,a tape (2) of the
entire proceedings,and a lovely
silver Mezuza,which he and Frieda are
to treasure.
Just one of those unforgettable
evenings.

Yes,it is Feb.21,1980. A second child is born to Carol and Ted
Trachtenberg. At his Brith,they name their son,Shlomo.

83

And it came to pass ....

...Hersh Schottenfeld took unto himself a wife, Ruchel, in Bolechow, Poland.
and they begot four sons - William, Isaac, Moisha, Selig, and a daughter Feiga

...and William took unto himself a wife from the family of Brown, Fanny,
and they begot three sons - Arthur, Louis, Nathan and a daughter Ruth.
and then William took unto himself a wife, Anna. Anna had a daughter Elsie
and William and Anna also begot a son Harold and a daughter Jean.

...and Arthur took unto himself a wife, Bessie and they begot two daughters, Elaine
and Linda

...and Nathan took unto himself a wife, Cappy.

...and Ruth took unto herself a husband from the family of Whitman, Lou,
and they begot a son Robert and a daughter Joan.

...and Elsie married and begot a daughter, Susan

...and Harold took unto himself a wife, Elaine. and they begot a son Steven and
a daughter Jan.

...and Jean took unto herself a husband, Jack. And they begot two daughters,
Laura and Kathy and a son Billy.

...and Isaac took unto himself a wife from the family of Hirshaut, Pippa.
and they begot four sons, William, Arthur, Louis and Harry and three daughters,
Ruth, Sarah and Hannah.

...and Ruth took unto herself a husband from the family of Kessler, Jack.
and they begot two daughters, Faye and Diana.
...and Faye took unto herself a husband from the family of Rosenfeld, Ronnie.
and they begot two sons, Harvey and Ira and a daughter Carol.
...and Harvey took unto himself a wife from the family of Waxman, Pamela.
...and Carol took unto herself a husband from the family of Trachtenberg, Theodore,
and they begot a daughter Shifra and a son Shlomo.
...and Diana took unto herself a husband from the family of Rosenblatt, Joel,
and they begot a daughter Cynthia and a son Jack.

...and William took himself a wife from the family of Steck, Lillian. And then
later from the family of Moscowitz, a wife Lillian Povidlo. Lillian has a family
and they have a son Jerry and a daughter Carol.
...and Jerry took unto himself Isabel, and they begot two sons, Arthur and Michael
and a daughter Bonnie.
...and Carol took unto herself a husband from the family of Weiss, Irving,
and they begot a son Bruce and a daughter Michelle.

84

...and Arthur took unto himself a wife from the family of Brooks, Lillian,
and they begot two daughters, Naomi and Rosalind and a son David.
...and Naomi took unto herself a husband from the family of Kudish, David,
and they begot a daughter Lisa and a son Seth.
...and Rosalind took unto herself a husband from the family of Schwartz, Alan.
...and David took unto himself a wife from the family of Wasserman, Ann,
and they begot a son Jason.

...and Louis took unto himself a wife from the family of Wilansky, Frieda,
and they begot two sons, Alan and Steven.
...and Alan took unto himself a wife from the family of Shuster, Aileene,
and they begot a daughter Lee.
...and Steven took unto himself a wife from the family of Florek, Joni.

...and Sarah took unto herself from the family of Berger a husband, Theodore,
and they begot a son Eugene and a daughter Ilene.

...and Harry took unto himself a wife from the family of Heisler, Florence,
and they begot a daughter Susan and a son Eric.

...and Hannah took unto herself a husband from the family of Levitz, Daniel,
and they begot two daughters, Judy and Fay and one son Fred.
...and Judy took unto herself a husband from the family of Karp, Ronnie,
and they begot a daughter Alana.
...and Fred took unto himself a wife from the family of Greene, Etty.

...and Moisha took himself from the family of Jampel, a wife, Fanny,
and they begot three daughters, Ruth, Gertrude and Mildred and one son, Sidney.

...and Ruth took unto herself a husband from the family of Teller, Jack,
and they begot one daughter Phyllis.
...and Phyllis took unto herself a husband from the family of Block, Richard,
and they begot two daughters, Sharon and Ellen.

...and Sidney took unto himself a wife from the family of Markowitz, Elayne,
and they begot two daughters, Faith and Ellen.

...and Jake took unto himself a wife from the family of Neuwirth, Fanny,
and they begot a daughter Ruth and a son Herbert.

...and Ruth took unto herself a husband from the family of Levine, Nat,
and they begot a son Barry and a daughter Sheryl.
...and Barry took unto himself a wife from the family of Kraf, Gail,
and they begot a son Steven and a daughter Suzanne.
...and Sheryl took unto herself a husband from the family of Graber, Marc,
and they begot a daughter Shawn and a son Ethan.

...and Herbert took unto himself a wife from the family of Balter, Lorraine.
and they begot four sons, Michael, Steven, Matthew and Howard.

...and Feiga took unto herself a husband from the family of Kornbluh, Max,
and they begot one son, Sidney and two daughters, Ruth and Shirley. Later, she
is take unto herself a husband from the family of Greifer, Morris.

...and Sidney took unto himself a wife from the family of Waxman, Tessie,
and they begot three sons, Martin, Alan and Gary.
...and Martin took unto himself a wife from the family of Horowitz, Natalie,
and they begot one daughter Lara and one son Alec.
...and Alan took unto himself a wife from the family of Lisoski, Charlene.

...and Ruth took unto herself a husband from the family of Zudiker, Hyman,
and they begot one son Michael and one daughter Ronnie.
...and Michael took unto himself a wife from the family of Russo, Mona,
and they begot one son, Steven.
...and Ronnie took unto herself a husband from the family of Zusman, Richard,
and they begot one son, Eric, and one daughter, Felicia.

...and Shirley took unto herself from the family of Diamond, a husband, Harold,
and they begot a son Merrill and a daughter Stephanie.
...and Merrill took unto himself from the family of Chotkowski, a wife, Karen.
...and Stephanie took unto herself a husband from the family of Horvitz, Ronnie.

...AND SO BEGAN THE GENERATIONS OF THE CLAN. OF THE
SCHOTTENFELD FAMILY CIRCLE.

...AND THEY WERE FRUITFUL - AND MULTIPLIED - AND IT WAS GOOD.

****

And, so we have caught up with the present day.
We, of the committee, hope you enjoyed your trip down memory lane.
We enjoyed assembling, discussing and working on the program.

Because of the great volume of pictures and facts, we had to
select just some of the events. Everything had to be fitted into
a time schedule.

If we had to leave out a favorite picture, or a favorite event,
please excuse us. Time did not permit its inclusion.

Yes, "This is your life", to the present day, The Schottenfeld
Family Circle.

The Committee,

Louis Schottenfeld

Frieda Schottenfeld

Ruth Zudiker

Narrators,   Hyman Zudiker

Ruth Levine   Herbert Schottenfeld

Louis Schottenfeld   Ruth Levine

Lorraine Schottenfeld   Nat Levine

Danny Levitz

CONCLUSION

This wonderful day, in Schottenfeld Family Circle history, has only been made possible because of the cooperation of all members, in sending photos, gathering dates of family events, and remembering things of interest that occurred in the past.

However, we would be amiss, if we did not mention some of those, who deserve a Medal of Honor, for doing things above and beyond the call of duty.

To Ruth Zudiker: for making a million calls gathering information, night or day-she never complained.

To Ruth Levine: for all that extra work in the Special Typing Category.

To Frieda Schottenfeld: for acting as unofficial secretary, in setting up meetings and calling for information needed.

To Ronnie Zusman: for making the original of the lovely invitations that were mailed.

To Ruth Teller: for gathering together priceless old photos, that were needed for background.

To Sarah Berger: for offering the wealth of photos and film she possessed.

To Hannah Levitz: for offering the wealth of photos and film she possessed.

To Lorraine Schottenfeld: for her suggestion on how to, best, bind the Journal and supplying the machine needed to do it.

we saved for last

To Herbert Schottenfeld: without whose efforts this evening would not have been possible:

for his work in splicing and assembling the film and slides to make a workable story.

for the gigantic task of getting this journal produced.

for his work in collating and binding the journal.

for his ideas on how best to present the program - coordinating the narrators, the film, the slides and the lighting.

All done because of love for the family and the family circle.

Herb, we salute you, and love you.

Louis B. Schottenfeld

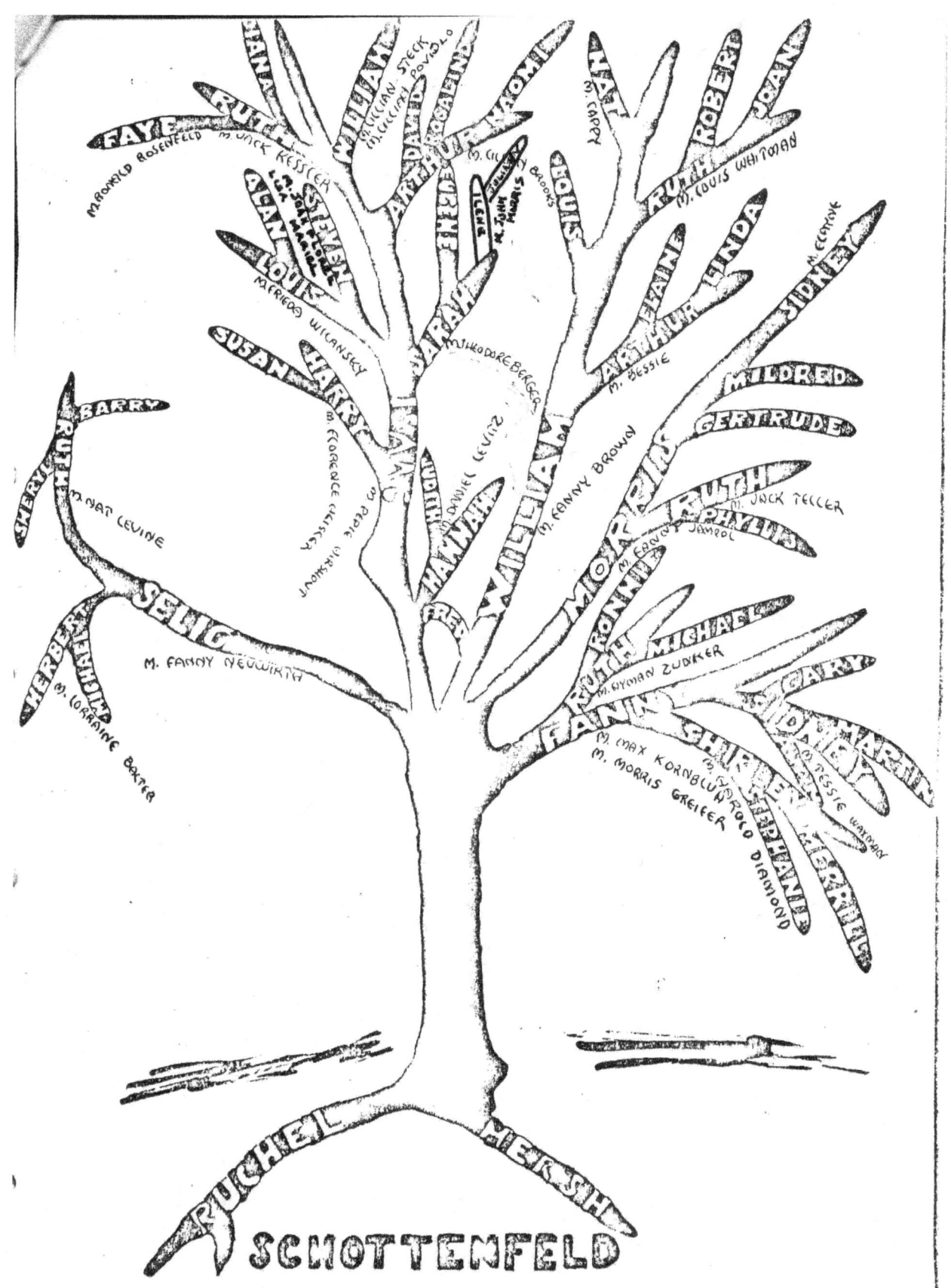

SCHOTTENFELD